REDISCOVERING JAPANESE BUSINESS LEADERSHIP

15 JAPANESE MANAGERS AND THE COMPANIES THEY'RE LEADING TO NEW GROWTH

REDISCOVERING JAPANESE BUSINESS LEADERSHIP

15 JAPANESE MANAGERS AND THE COMPANIES THEY'RE LEADING TO NEW GROWTH

YOZO HASEGAWA

TRANSLATED BY TONY KIMM

WILEY

John Wiley & Sons (Asia) Pte. Ltd.

Other Wiley Editorial Offices
John Wiley & Sons, 111 River Street, Hoboken, NJ 07030, USA
John Wiley & Sons, The Atrium, Southern Gate, Chichester, West Sussex, P019 8SQ,
    United Kingdom
John Wiley & Sons (Canada) Ltd., 5353 Dundas Street West, Suite 400, Toronto, Ontario,
    M9B 6HB, Canada
John Wiley & Sons Australia Ltd., 42 McDougall Street, Milton, Queensland 4064,
    Australia
Wiley-VCH, Boschstrasse 12, D-69469 Weinheim, Germany

Library of Congress Cataloging-in-Publication Data
ISBN 978-0-470-82495-5

Typeset in 10.5/13 Sabon Roman by MPS Limited, A Macmillan Company
Printed in Singapore by Saik Wah Press Pte. Ltd.
10 9 8 7 6 5 4 3 2 1

CONTENTS

PREFACE

Japanese business has changed tremendously in the past decade. Once sacred institutions such as lifetime employment and seniority-based promotion in the workplace have increasingly been replaced by "temp" contracts and performance-based pay. During Japan's miracle growth years in the two decades following the end of World War II, the nation's schools churned out a veritable "soldier" class of white-collared *sarariman* (salaried men) and OLs (office ladies) dedicated to building their country into an economic superpower. And they succeeded. They toiled long hours with little complaint until their identities became nearly inseparable from those of their companies. In exchange for this loyalty, companies provided them with lifetime job security and benefits, lifelong drinking buddies and access to company retreats. People were indeed the country's richest natural resource.

Under the protection of the US–Japan Security Treaty, the entire country could concentrate its energies on making things. The government encouraged key industries, facilitated exports, built a modern national infrastructure, and engendered the rise of a consumer-based middle-class society.

Within a generation of its devastating defeat in World War II, Japan had risen from shambles into the second-largest economy on the planet. But then came the oil crises of the 1970s, followed by higher valuation of the yen in the early 1980s and the tremendous burst of an asset price bubble at the dawn of the 1990s. The age of limitless expansion had come to an end. As the world entered into the twenty-first century, newly emerging economic powerhouses such as China and India looked to replace advanced industrialized countries of the West, among whom Japan was included, as the new manufacturing centers and drivers of global growth.

Confronting an aging population and shrinking demand at home, Japan seemed to be headed back toward a more middling ranking among world powers. Yet Japan still boasted some of the largest, most advanced and well-recognized companies the world had ever known; companies whose technological sophistication and business practices continued to serve as models and mentors to newly emerging nations. Leading Japanese businesses had in short outgrown their home market, and not simply in the manufacturing sector. They needed a bigger pond to swim in, and saw renewed opportunities in the advancement of information technology (IT), the globalization of markets, and increasing pressures for global society to meet environmental and sustainability challenges.

Japanese companies are regaining some of their past spotlight and discovering a new swagger amid structural changes taking place in the global economic landscape. Although the large automotive and electronics manufacturers, long the primary drivers of Japan's export-led growth, have all been hit hard by shrinking demand and stiffer competition around the world, those very same conditions have also allowed the rise of a new group of business leaders and companies, hailing from broader segments of the economy, including entertainment, apparel, and food. Out of both necessity and ambition, a greater variety of Japanese companies are now eagerly looking to contribute more to the world than sophisticated but faceless mechanical devices, seeking instead to capitalize on the growing universal appeal for different lifestyle aesthetics and values.

Meanwhile, the country's key manufacturing industries—automotive, machinery, electronics, and steel—continue working to reinvent themselves and strengthen their relevance in the world by churning out value-added products and cutting-edge technologies. They have also begun to capitalize on their early presence in the emerging markets of Asia.

Nearly all the companies treated in this book have recalibrated their global expansion initiatives to focus on, if not begin in, the East. If they can make the most of their know-how and technological strengths, Japanese companies should find ways to grow and evolve alongside these emerging economies as cooperative partners in what has become the growth center of the world.

My primary aim for this book, therefore, is to expound on some of the key strategies, philosophies, and principles at work among top managers at 15 of Japan's most promising—and enduring—companies as they seek to reach new plateaus of growth and global leadership in the twenty-first century. Through direct interviews I have had with many of the business leaders featured in this book, along with research, data verification and reference to official announcements, as well as knowledge accumulated over a 40-year career at Japan's leading business newspaper, the *Nihon Keizai Shimbun*, I hope to shed some light on what some of the best business minds in Japan are thinking about today.

While I focus on the current leaders of 15 companies that I believe best represent the future of Japanese industry, a quick glance at the names of those companies will surely evoke Japan's glorious past as well. This is a major theme of this book. For whether it is the reform effort of an exemplary leader or a company's culturally engrained legacy for change, all these companies have proven eminently capable of overcoming crisis after crisis to emerge stronger and more committed to a brighter future than before.

The companies and managers I discuss in this book include global game software sensation Nintendo Co., rapidly up-and-coming apparel company Fast Retailing (Uniqlo); and consumer lifestyle companies such as Seven & i Holdings, Secom Co. (security), and Yamato Holdings (transport), all of which have achieved stable growth in earnings and high levels of consumer trust through repeated reforms.

There are also traditional companies such as Kirin Holdings (beverages), Shiseido Co. (cosmetics), Kikkoman Corporation (food) and Takeda Pharmaceutical Co., which are rapidly on their way to becoming globally managed entities. Finally, I talk about leading manufacturers Toyota Motor Corporation, Panasonic Corporation, Canon Inc., Nippon Steel Corporation, Komatsu Ltd., and Toray Industries, Inc., which are looking to reinforce their competitive strengths through advanced technologies and a stronger global presence.

While all of these companies have repeatedly demonstrated their aptitude to overcome crises and emerge more competitive through great persistence, adaptability, and constant self-improvement, what many of these Japanese firms are also seeing amid an unprecedented global recession is a need to return to homegrown business values.

In an effort to compete on an equal footing in an increasingly borderless world, Japanese companies for years had sought to adopt or mimic more "Western" business models that emphasized speed and short-term results. Now, however, managers are coming full circle and realizing that what may best serve their interests on the global stage as well as at home is a return to more traditional Japanese business values and practices that include a predisposition to a long-term view, a continued craftsperson-like devotion to quality and scrupulous attention to detail, management continuity and consensus, the primacy of the workplace or shopfloor, the steady-but-sure accretion of results, and the need for constant improvement efforts.

While these qualities may not often lead to punctuated leaps in technology or the sudden transformations that can catapult a company to overnight success, they have long proven to be the hallmarks of a Japanese business ethos and culture wherein respect for tradition and human relations remain high-priority values.

This is not to say that Japanese firms haven't been hard hit by the global financial crisis of 2008–09. Toyota Motor Corporation is posting unprecedented losses even as it has ascended to number one automaker in the world. It will take considerable time and some hearty reforms for many of these companies to recover their strong positive earnings. As Akio Toyoda described in his advocacy of a more "lifesized" style of management, most Japanese companies have only to take better measure of their special skills and strengths to effectively invest the technological prowess and human intellectual capital they wield into products and services of higher quality and performance than those of their lower-cost competitors. In this way, they can play a leading role in meeting new twenty-first-century needs while shaping the global economy for years to come.

I believe if the companies in this book, along with so many others that I regrettably could not treat this time around, truly begin to maximize their technological and intellectual assets, particularly in the environmental sphere, and prove capable of adapting their traditional business values into global models of success, then I see no reason any of these companies should not be able to thrive in the future, if not lead the way through it.

I therefore hope that through this book, you will be able to get a feeling for what constitutes some of the strengths of contemporary Japanese management and companies so that it may add some color to your perspective on the new economic paradigm unfolding before us.

Finally, I would like to express my deepest thanks to Sho Kambara for his help in writing this book, and warmest gratitude to the managers and public relations directors at the companies treated in this book for their generous and unsparing cooperation.

Yozo Hasegawa
January 2010

1

SUCCEEDING BY DESTROYING A GROWTH MODEL

Kanemasa Haraguchi
Executive Vice Chairman
Secom Co., Ltd.

Born August 1950, Kyoto. Graduated March 1974 from Musashino Institute of Technology (renamed Tokyo City University) with a degree in telecommunications engineering from the engineering department. Joined Nihon Keibi Hosho K.K. (renamed Secom Co., Ltd.) in April 1974. Appointed vice-president in 2002, president in 2005 and executive vice chairman in January 2010. Viewed as both managerial and spiritual successor to company founder, Makoto Iida, with the technocratic background to lead the company to new prosperity and growth in the information age.

Always Re-examine Your Values

Personal security is a relatively new concept in Japan. Long considered one of the safest countries in the world, Japan had until recent years managed to avoid the rising crime rates that had accompanied industrial development in many of its Western counterparts. Social scientists like to point to a variety of factors for this, including relative income equality and stability, near homogeneity of race—which breeds shared norms and mores—and social behavior dictated less by religious beliefs or universal codes of conduct than by the particular demands and exigencies of sustaining harmony in the small groupings to which people belong, such as family, schools, neighborhoods, and places of employment. People moved in relatively small social circles; and that perhaps more than anything else may have reinforced the day-to-day standards of propriety and moral guidance to feed and maintain social order.

But with the advance of globalization, freer movement of goods, services, and particularly labor, this once relatively isolated island country is gradually evolving into a more open and pluralistic citizen of the world. Greater mobility, as well as increasing diversity of demand and lifestyles and Japan's shrinking population, in particular, augur perhaps greater immigration in the coming years to sustain the country's social and economic infrastructure. With increased plurality of interests and values, and growing detachment or accountability to local social circles, individual and impersonal crimes motivated more by self-interest and economic gain than by malfunctioning relationships have been on a steady incline in Japan.

Security, in a variety of forms, is therefore a growth industry. But security against crime is only part of the story in a country that is rapidly aging. Companies such as Secom that are on top of the changes taking place in the country demographically and economically are finding themselves constantly expanding and refining the meaning of their businesses as they seek to overcome new challenges and exploit new opportunities, both at home and abroad.

Secom company founder Makoto Iida is widely credited as the founding father of the security industry in Japan. Iida was the fifth son of a sake merchant in one of Tokyo's oldest quarters, Nihombashi, and the Iida family had gained a modest level of local respect as a supplier of spirits and beverages to restaurants and guesthouses.

Because Makoto was the fifth son, he was exempt from any expectations of one day taking over the family business, and therefore grew up largely free and unfettered. His parents even encouraged him to actively pursue his every interest. They didn't spoil him, but insisted that he have a serious and active approach to whatever he did, and possess meaningful objectives.

Iida recalls as a youngster being severely reprimanded by his father for merely walking with his head down, or crouching lackadaisically in public. To his father, it was a disgrace to appear publicly as downcast and aimless.

Indeed, Iida's father was a man of open and forthright disposition, and was always lecturing his children about the role that one's psychology has in affecting what happens in real life.

On another occasion, Iida recalls his mother admonishing him for sighing in exasperation. "When you sigh, you allow happiness to escape," she told him. The young Iida found something very convincing and fathomable about that imagery, and says he has been mindful of sighing ever since.

Owing to the accessible wisdom imparted by his parents, Iida grew up generally trusting the counsel of adults. But it wasn't a blind universal trust. Otherwise, how could he eventually pioneer a business that was implicitly built around a suspicion of trust, much less rise to the top of that industry?

Safety is Not Free

> It's a good thing that a business can fail. Because if I knew someone would come in and save it, I would lose the ability to manage with any suspense at all.

This quote perhaps best captures the personality and business philosophy of Makoto Iida. Iida treats risk as a given. Everyone has their share of both successes and failures, and Iida believes that any business action is predicated upon an acknowledgment and embracing of risk. "If all you do is stick to what is safe, there is little incentive to act with any resolve and you diffuse any expectation of progress."

Iida indeed undertook an immense risk in deciding to build a business out of something that had long been considered free: peace of mind. He believed that greater safety and security, and consequently peace of mind, could be purchased. As mentioned at the outset of this chapter, the security business is still quite young in Japan, at least as a private sector endeavor. The government, of course, provided public security through the national police force. But with the exception of providing against some external threat, most Japanese prided themselves on the notion that theirs was for the most part a "safe, peaceful and orderly" country; one where people implicitly respected each other's possessions and privacy. Safety was therefore taken for granted, like oxygen. Offering security as a commercial commodity never really occurred to anyone as necessary or desirable.

Perhaps much of the nation was too busy rebuilding their country after their defeat in World War II to think about protecting what little they had. By the early 1960s, when disparities in material wealth were beginning to emerge, Makoto Iida took notice of the rising number of reported crimes each year, and began thinking that "eventually, the time would come when Japan, too, would see peace of mind security as something to be purchased."

Public safety—to be distinguished from private security—was the domain of the police, who were stationed in local police booths in every community across the country. They conducted local censuses, patrolled neighborhoods on foot or on bicycles, helped people with directions, and even on occasion lent out cash. To their credit, they still do all of this. But there have always been those nooks and crannies that inevitably escape or exceed their reach. It is precisely those areas that Iida saw as increasingly vulnerable to exploitation, particularly on private or commercial property.

Iida believed that if he could offer an added level of safety and peace of mind as a service, there must surely be businesses that would feel the need for it. So at 29, Iida ignored the many naysayers around him and established the *Keibi Hosho* ("security guarantee") company, forerunner to Secom Co., Ltd.

Iida's vision proved prescient. As Japan grew into the world's second-richest nation, followed by growing demands for home-market liberalization, deregulation, and freer immigration, new types of crime emerged alongside existing ones, as did their frequency and intensity. Thus followed a dramatic increase in business demand for protective and preventive security measures.

Secom grew into the largest provider of private security systems, for both corporate clients and households, with a whopping 60 percent share of a market that is currently swamped with some 10,000 rival companies, large and small, across the nation.

Be Mindful of Constant Changes in Your Situation

Iida's venture began with a suspicion that Japan's reputation as the world's safest country was either a myth or a phenomenon that simply couldn't last. He then parlayed that foresight into a new kind of business that proved adept at mining a hidden demand and winning acceptance. But he didn't act on a whim. Iida may have gone with his gut instinct in coming up with a business premise, but he then looked to verify it through extensive research before ultimately coming to a decision. Even so, he met with stiff resistance.

The secret to Iida's entrepreneurial strength lay in his acceptance of risk in a forthright pursuit of an interest that he viewed as having meaningful objectives. This is precisely what his parents had taught him, and it served him well, as he found himself running a company that was riding the crest of changing times.

Secom continues to run far ahead of the curve, and its competition. One of those reasons has to do with current company president, Kanemasa Haraguchi, who is viewed as a natural successor to Iida and the right leader for carrying forward and building upon the founder's philosophy.

Since becoming Secom president in 2004, Haraguchi has taken a business that owed its remarkable growth primarily to corporate security services, and aggressively worked to expand demand for its services to a still largely untapped market for individual security. While Iida had moved the focus of the company's services away from manned security (security guards) to IT-based systems, Haraguchi has worked to strengthen programs that build and maintain strong human resources as the surest way to sustain a high level of service quality.

"I feel the strong influence of our founder, Makoto Iida, every day," says Haraguchi. "That is because his beliefs are embodied in the Secom philosophy itself, such as always endeavoring to do what you believe is right and never flinching from new challenges, both of which may require you to break with the past. This is why instead of apprehensions, there are high expectations inside our company that we are embarking upon a brilliant new chapter in our history as we embrace the rapid changes and opportunities of the information age."

Haraguchi is clear about what will keep Secom viable going forward:

> One is people, and the other is technology. These are two strengths that will enable Secom to respond to these difficult and changing times. Our products and services are all provided by Secom people. They are the reason we don't believe in out-sourcing. We rely instead on having highly capable people who carry out their work responsibly and with full understanding of who we are, where we've come from, and what we stand for. We don't believe you can succeed with a model based on the easy interchangeability of people. Because that is precisely what will lose you the trust of your customers.

When Secom was awarded the job of providing security to athletes during the 1964 Tokyo Olympics, just two years after the company's inception, it was a breakout moment. The sudden exposure Secom received was tremendous, and most of the Japanese public had been unfamiliar with the very concept of the business. With the Olympic games, private security entered the national consciousness to such a degree that Secom served as a model for a popular television miniseries the next year about the life of a security guard. Until then, the job of a security guard, and the security business over-all, had either gone largely unnoticed or struck people as a peculiar novelty.

Shrinking a Growth Business by Design

It was precisely when business was soaring and the sky seemed the limit when Secom founder, Makoto Iida, decided to raise a red flag. His trusted successor, Haraguchi, can attest to that:

> Iida has never been one to feel completely satisfied or comfortable with success. Instead, he can't help but continually question himself and his actions, which is why he stunned everybody when he announced that we needed to rethink the business from the ground up. Despite our company's readiness to change, he again met with strong internal resistance. Basically, he proposed that we change our business model from one that relied largely on on-site guards to one focused on security services through telecommunications technology. This stirred up heated internal debate over what that would mean exactly, and what level of genuine security Secom could promise to our customers by reducing on-site personnel. But Iida strongly asserted that no matter how successful a business you may have, you must constantly be aware that the times will change without your consent, and you must adapt or you will face obsolescence.

Secom at the time of the announcement had a workforce of sev-eral thousand employees. Iida was convinced that if it continued on a linear trajectory, the company's survival would only become increasingly threatened with the emergence of more competitors following similar models.

"Viewed in hindsight, it was the right move," remarks Iida. "But at the time, the general telecom infrastructure was not amply in place in Japan, so we began by having to install dedicated lines of our own. Though costly, the advantage was that nobody else was doing it. So we were able to gain considerable lead time over our competitors, and able to keep coming up with new ideas to leverage that lead."

Behind this change in management policy, by all measures quite revolutionary, lay a fundamental precept in Iida's business philosophy:

> There comes a point in time when it is right and appropriate to squarely face something that you achieved with the most single-minded belief, effort, and conviction, and be prepared to reject it. Otherwise, nothing truly new will ever be born.

One has to be driven by either tremendous courage or supreme folly to want to dismantle a successful business model that has taken years to build. But Iida, in his inimitable penchant for self-examination, found himself once again questioning some basic assumptions about his business. Instead of relying on the availability of physical manpower—in the form of security guards making the rounds—couldn't the same if not better level of security services be provided by some means that wasn't so labor intensive? The answer, of course, was the development of telecom infrastructure.

A greater focus on technology was precisely what Secom needed to catapult it into the next century. The shape of crime, too, was changing, growing more sophisticated and more pervasive. And security services needed to be a step ahead of that change.

For example, Secom developed video technology to detect and record intrusions in high clarity, even in pitch darkness, and then automatically feed that information to a Secom monitoring center. To prevent intrusions where the perpetrator dresses up as, say, a parcel delivery person to gain entry into a building, Secom has been developing a visual intercom system with built-in facial recognition functionality. If no match is made, an alarm is sounded.

"We're also developing ways to distinguish between reliable and unreliable information over networks," says Haraguchi. "We need to continue to enhance our network security services as new needs and realities of the information age arise, or better yet, to pre-empt them."

In short, Makoto Iida's gambit paid off; his read on the future once again proved prescient. The field of computer and sensor technologies that he steered the company into as a replacement for a staff-intensive model set the company down a path that would soon be followed by the advent of something called "IT."

Adapting to a Changing, Aging Society

The twice reinvented Secom is now extending its reach into another and wholly different space. It is the field of health care. Japan is the world's most rapidly aging society. It is estimated that by 2015, one in four people in the country will be over the age of 65. The birth rate, by contrast, has been declining for 34 years. While this presents a host of serious social and economic challenges for the country, it also offers a significant business opportunity for companies like Secom.

Secom has begun partnering with medical institutions to offer individual customers emergency medical assistance call services using its existing security systems. This has also led to entry into the field of nursing care, such as health care services and pay nursing homes, of which there are far too few service providers to satisfy current and projected demand.

All of this is rapidly broadening the scope and definition of security, though still within the conceptual realm of providing "peace of mind."

"Security is not just about protecting people from thieves and burglars, but anything that can pose a threat to human life and family welfare," Haraguchi opines. "As we confront the growing needs of an aging society, it is incumbent on us to provide comprehensive security services that not only protect people from crime, but also improve their access to other aspects of their daily welfare, such as nursing care and medical treatment."

While Secom on the one hand appears to have found itself blessed by a series of natural growth opportunities, in truth, the company's progress has been spearheaded by a keen sensitivity and genuine responsiveness to real changes in people's lives, embodied of course in the philosophy of Makoto Iida and Kanemasa Haraguchi. Secom's foray into health care is a risky one that could sap energy and strength away from its core security services, which have ensured continued growth and stable earnings since the founding. But risk is a given, and so is change. Secom's penchant to honor the founder's venture spirit, even as the leader of its industry, has given rise to a vibrant business perspective, and continues to keep Secom on the cutting edge. Haraguchi believes health care is on a trajectory to become a billion-dollar industry in the near future, and Secom plans to play a major role in comprehensively supporting the health, safety, and security of people's lives, while not necessarily from cradle to grave, perhaps from living room to downtown offices and all the spaces in between.

Greater Growth in "Security"

When asked whether his company's success so far can be credited to getting an early jump on the IT age, Haraguchi says "no:"

> To be sure, IT enabled us to undergo an incredible transformation. At the time, there wasn't any particular strategy formed around IT, per se. Our thinking was more in tune with asking the important question: Do we have sufficient skepticism right now even in the midst of great success to keep us capable of responding to the next big change down the road? It won't matter if we have access to the most wonderful technologies and human talent known to man, if we err in the use and timing in which to apply them, it will be tantamount to never having known them at all. That's why a person or a company that cannot swim with the current of the times will always be gobbled up, no matter what age you live in.

This is an all-important question for Secom, which is constantly being called upon to bolster the range and sophistication of its products and services to meet new needs. One example is the rash of crimes that began around 2004, in which gullible, often elderly, citizens are tricked into depositing money into unknown accounts at automated teller machines (ATMs). Often, it will begin with a telephone call from someone pretending to be a family member in need of money, or a fictitious claim for some unpaid bill or service. The perpetrator only need provide a bank account number into which the victim is instructed to deposit money, and the transaction is completed. Often, the caller is guiding the victim by telephone at the ATM machine. Secom has been called upon to beef up security and prevention systems across the country to combat this kind of fraud at teller machines.

Twelve Countries and Counting

What about Secom overseas? Social and demographic conditions vary greatly between countries and regions, but surely good technology and systems can travel anywhere.

Secom is pursuing a concerted overseas expansion strategy, and already operates in 12 countries, including Australia and the UK, and with a particularly strong presence in Asian countries including South Korea, China, Thailand, Singapore, and Chinese Taipei.

Secom launched the first online security system in Taiwan in 1978 through a technical and management tieup that led to the creation of Taiwan Secom Co. Similar to Secom's early days in Japan, it was an idea that began with very little traction. There were very few companies that saw the need for, much less understood the concept of, buying safety. So, as in Japan, Secom salespeople made the rounds one company at a time, persuading them as to the value of the service, and slowly building up a client base. Eventually, Secom's security systems gained penetration and understanding in the form of increasing contracts until finally growing to a stockmarket listing in 1993, and paving the way for a burgeoning security industry in Taiwan. From there, the number of contracts increased to the point where today Secom offers its safety products and services to more than 100,000 clients.

Taiwan Secom currently has 80 business offices, 2,300 employees, and since its founding has maintained top share of the private security business in Taiwan as a blue chip company.

A joint venture with the Samsung Group in 1981 established Secom in the South Korean market through a company that was later renamed S1 Corporation. Again, this was the first private, online security systems provider in the country.

Korea was at the height of a rapid economic growth drive that had begun in the 1970s, but it still took time for the private security idea to be completely understood. As with the Tokyo Olympics in 1964, the big breakthrough came in 1986 and 1988, with Korea's holding of the Asian Games followed by the summer Olympic Games in Seoul, respectively. South Korea used these two games as a platform to show the world that it had joined the ranks of the world's leading economic powers, and with the growth and arrival of new and global businesses and financial institutions, so grew a need for what Secom and S1 had to offer, along with acknowledgment that Secom was already a high-quality provider in the field. In 1996, S1 was listed on the Korean stock exchange, and began offering home security systems as well.

S1 maintains a near 60 percent share of the online security systems market in Korea. Secom stickers can be seen everywhere, so much so that the name Secom has become synonymous with "security systems."

Even rival companies can be heard proffering their services to prospective clients by saying, "Would you like to install a Secom?" S1 has 360,000 accounts and is tops among the more than 2,000 private security solutions companies in Korea. It is a significant contributor to the Secom Group.

Like most corporate global strategies, China is the overseas market that is drawing the most current attention. Secom entered Beijing in 1992 with the establishment of Secom (China) Co. The next year, it formed a joint venture with a Dalian firm to start China's first online security system for corporate clients.

Since then, it has set up companies in Beijing, Qingdao, Shanghai, and Shenzhen, targeting local and Japanese businesses. Each of those companies has in turn set up branches or other companies in surrounding regions to expand the market. The next step is to establish and expand bases in principal inland cities.

Secom has succeeded in earning very high plaudits overseas and is enjoying rapid growth in contracts. A large part of that success, Haraguchi says, is due to a commitment to localism:

> As we seek to raise awareness of the Secom brand in the Asian region, and expand our business there, it is indispensable that we cooperate with and train local staff who know their home markets better than we do. We won't succeed otherwise. Problems are bound to occur among staff due to cultural and philosophical differences. So it's not enough to pound the pavement. We need to foster highly trained, capable people. Only then can we expect to be able to provide high-quality security services.

Secom is also moving briskly ahead into Thailand, Malaysia, Singapore, Indonesia, Vietnam, and Australia. With more than 550,000 contracts overseas, there is still plenty of room to grow when compared to the more than 1.2 million contracts in Japan. But building a society where people can improve their quality of life in complete safety and peace of mind is something desired by all people of the world. Haraguchi says, making that wish come true is Secom's mission:

> We don't want people to purchase our products simply because it's better to be safe than sorry. No, we want them to feel completely gratified for having come to us because they're getting

a level of support, security, and peace of mind that goes far beyond just a buffer against crime or mishap. A good service business has to offer a lot of intangibles as well; the know-how, creativity, and expertise to meet customer needs and wishes fully, and a desire to be a strong beacon or positive force in the community.

From Korea to India, Secom actively seeks to promote exchanges among its younger constituents along with technology exchanges. This active approach to growth in Asia, Haraguchi believes, is an investment sure to provide enormous dividends in the future.

While Secom may have pioneered the security industry and earned top share in some of those countries, total consolidated earnings overseas still only account for only about 4 percent of earnings garnered at home. This is one reason Haraguchi believes the company must devote increasing energy and resources to expansion in overseas markets. But it must be done prudently. Secom did not acquire its large customer base in Japan overnight, but built up its business gradually and by overcoming its share of tough hurdles. He expects to earn market share abroad in much the same way.

There is a commonly held belief among business watchers that service sector companies from Japan are just not well suited to business overseas. Manufacturers, on the other hand, are. But that notion ignores that Secom is already a leading security service company in 12 other countries beside Japan. A primary reason is, as stated earlier, that Secom does not sell itself as a Japanese company in those countries. Instead, it partners with local companies for joint business development in those markets, where Secom is then viewed as a local service provider:

Each region in Japan has its own culture and ways of thinking. That's even more pronounced when you go abroad. For Japanese to attempt to transfer products and services designed for the Japanese market to other countries without conforming them accordingly would be not only time consuming and difficult but a recipe for failure. That is why we partner with local companies who understand their communities. We can provide the systems and technologies that we have developed and have proven to be effective, but locals need to decide how best to deploy them.

Despite a global recession, Secom continues to post record sales and profits. One could say that Secom is thriving because these are incredibly trying times, and people are more sensitive to both real and perceived threats to their security.

But economic fears notwithstanding, Secom sees considerable room to grow both overseas, and in health care. The most immediate growth potential lies in the household security market. Households constitute fewer than 40 percent of Secom's security service contracts, but demand has been growing twice as fast as for corporate contracts, particularly in metropolitan areas. The countryside remains largely untapped.

Summary: Security in a Changing World

Despite incredible economic volatility in the world, Secom has succeeded in sustaining a solid and stable revenue base thanks in large part to a business model involving long-term customer subscriptions. Once equipment is installed, it is difficult and costly for a business or a condominium to readily make wholesale changes, but with the proper follow-up services by Secom, there is little need to. Secom founder, Makoto Iida, remains an active behind-the-scenes advisor who can ensure that the venture spirit of this still relatively young enterprise remains vibrant and relevant while also encouraging a corporate culture that enthusiastically embraces fresh opportunities.

"Our customers have put in our care the keys to their safety," says Iida. "It is our responsibility to therefore respond to their trust and continually seek to improve their security and peace of mind through improvements and added value."

Iida's business model began with corporate security contracts. He sought to earn such a high level of trust from business customers as "watchdog" over their property that "security" would come to be treated as a justifiable and natural expense, and thereby secure for Secom a stable source of revenue. With the increase in households where both marriage partners work and leave their homes vacant for most of the day, Iida identified a new need for home security, and developed a business model for homes and condominiums. This demand has been further accelerated with Japan's rapidly aging population as more and more elderly find themselves living alone, and must rely on various cleaning, nursing care, and delivery services, all of which require better and more replete home security support.

Secom has gone from a visionary startup company premised on a perceived future need for purchasable "safety" to a company capable of sustaining growth and evolving with the changing times, as evidenced by its shift from staff-based to so-called mechanical-based security, and expansion from corporate to individual subscribers. Now, Secom is examining ways to grow in Asia and other markets abroad.

For the longest time, President Kanemasa Haraguchi kept his desk in a corner of Makoto Iida's office for a specific reason. Whenever Iida would come up with a new idea, Haraguchi would immediately commit it to paper and draft a quick feasibility plan to send off into the field for practical feedback. From this experience, Haraguchi says he has come to know Iida's philosophy and can almost guess what his founder will think of next. Above all, Haraguchi says, he has learned the basics of growing a business. If Iida is the wellspring of Secom's venture spirit, then perhaps Haraguchi is its leading missionary.

In contrast to Makoto Iida, who was born into an enterprising family and is at heart a philosopher, Haraguchi's background is more technocratic. He majored in electronic and communications engineering and possesses a more digital way of thinking. He can insert technical footnotes to Iida's ideas, fleshing out conceptual blueprints.

Quite fortuitously, Haraguchi joined Secom just as Iida's emphasis on the business was shifting away from static guard security to mechanical security services. The business was about to enter an age of large computerized control systems, making Haraguchi's value to the company as a tech-savvy manager that much more valuable.

In short, Iida and Secom co-founder Juichi Toda chose to relinquish day-to-day management at just the right time, and to just the right person. With a strong earnings mechanism already in place, Iida retired from the front lines knowing that he had done what was needed to establish a corporate culture that would continue to approach new business opportunities with the venture spirit he believed so important.

The role of President Haraguchi is now to expand the depth and breadth of automated security that Iida pioneered, and open up new markets, all the while cherishing the template for success bequeathed to him by the founder. He must make the business model fit the demands of the market and the times, and then seek to make it work universally. Secom's move into emergency medical response business is but one example.

Secom had its thirty-seventh consecutive year of growth in sales and operating profit in 2009, with all divisions showing a positive balance, and record sales and operating profit for the fiscal year ending March 2009.

Consistent and steady management has long been one of the distinctive hallmarks of Japanese business, and Secom has increasingly come to be seen in recent years as a living example. Just as it happened in Japan, new value is being attached to notions of safety and security in other parts of Asia as those economies develop, and there is little reason to doubt that Secom will play a larger role in bringing peace of mind to the world at large.

Principal Ideas of Makoto Iida and Kanemasa Haraguchi

- When trying something new, you invariably need to discard something old.
- Always doubt the success of your business. It will help prepare you for the change and crises ahead.
- People or organizations incapable of moving with the times have always been left behind.

Secom Co., Ltd.

Established: July 7, 1962
Kanemasa Haraguchi, Executive Vice Chairman
Makoto Iida, Founder and Executive Advisor
Head office: 1-5-1, Jingumae, Shibuya-ku, Tokyo
http://www.secom.co.jp/english/
Capital: 66,300 million yen (year ending March 31, 2009)
Consolidated sales: 678,400 million yen
Consolidated operating profit: 87,634 million yen
Consolidated net profit: 21,502 million yen
Employees: 34,078

2

IN THE RIGHT PLACE, GOOD THINGS SELL THEMSELVES

Toshifumi Suzuki
Chairman and CEO
Seven & i Holdings Co., Ltd.

Born December 1932 in Nagano Prefecture, Japan. Graduated 1956 from the Faculty of Economics at Chuo University and entered major publishing distribution firm, Tokyo Shuppan Hanbai (currently Tohan Corporation), working there for six years before joining the super-market chain, Ito-Yokado Company in 1962. In 1973, Suzuki was instrumental in the launch of convenience store chain, 7-Eleven Japan, as an Ito-Yokado subsidiary, and has held titles no lower than president and representative director of that company since 1978, in addition to various other posts including president of Ito-Yokado from 1992. Suzuki has been chairman and chief executive officer of Seven & i Holdings since 2005 and was responsible for the introduction of the POS (point-of-sale) inventory monitoring system deployed through-out 7-Eleven and Ito-Yokado stores. Suzuki established revolutionary new procurement and sales methodologies based on consumer needs, and helped create the world's largest and most successful convenience store franchise chain.

Turning Something Free Into a Marketable Product

"7-Eleven is the best!"

That was the ebullient reaction of one young college student to another as they emerged from a newly opened 7-Eleven store in their neighborhood. Both held a loaf of bread, given out free with any purchase to first-day customers.

A blogger, posting about things to do and see in his Tokyo neighborhood, wrote triumphantly, "Finally! We get a 7-Eleven in the neighborhood!"

Never mind that there were other convenience stores within short walking distance in several directions, and another 7-Eleven store no more than 10 minutes away on foot. The distance between convenience stores in most urban and suburban settings in Japan can be measured in mere yards. Everyone almost invariably has a choice.

There were estimated to be some 40,000 convenience stores across Japan at the end of 2008, and 12,000 of them (30 percent) are 7-Eleven. While the top four convenience store chains combined account for roughly 80 percent of the market, 7-Eleven still nearly doubles its second-largest competitor in number of stores.

Since it arrived on Japanese shores, 7-Eleven has proven itself the runaway leader in a rapidly growing retail sector. So it should come as no surprise that the person who brought this company to such commanding heights, Toshifumi Suzuki, is also the man responsible for growing the nation's largest retail conglomerate, Seven & i Holdings.

When 7-Eleven was launched in Japan in 1973, the location chosen for its inaugural store was Toyosu, a busy industrial district built on landfill in Tokyo's Koto Ward. It was a small shop and its opening went relatively unheralded. But by the next year when 24-hour business began at the Toramaru store in Koriyama City, Fukushima Prefecture, 7-Eleven Japan had, in just a year, added 100 stores to its name. It has since grown into an enormous franchise of 5,500 employees and annual sales of 2.7 trillion yen.

Much of this success is attributed to the incredible business instincts, savvy and vision of Toshifumi Suzuki, a man who had entered the retail industry at 30 after switching careers.

Suzuki started in publishing, at Japan's largest bookseller and distributor, Tokyo Shuppan Hanbai, (renamed Tohan). But he nurtured dreams of becoming a journalist. Upon graduating from Chuo University, Suzuki felt his vocational aspirations coming to fruition as he was given an informal offer from a major publishing company, only to find to his great astonishment upon graduating that the offer had been rescinded.

"This simply isn't right," Suzuki had protested. But he was forced to try a different tack. He started fishing around for a more indirect route into publishing. If publishing companies didn't want to hire him, perhaps he could find work with a major book distributor, to which all publishers basically had to kowtow if they wanted to see their books sold. And so he found employment at Japan's largest book distributor, Tokyo Shuppan, or Tohan Corp., for short.

Suzuki didn't have many opportunities at Tohan to cultivate his journalistic skills, but he did happen upon the company's free in-house weekly newsletter, which was distributed to bookstores. It was little more than an announcement of the latest book releases, but Suzuki decided to try turning it into readable literature, and began attaching self-penned articles to the release announcements. Before long, the value of the content outgrew its free status.

Suzuki started commissioning writers, while still contributing articles himself. He revamped the publication's layout and cover, and oversaw its growth in circulation from a paltry 5,000 to 130,000 issues. One thing Suzuki noticed was that "free" often carried an association among consumers as being of no utility or value. But the moment a price tag was affixed to something, people craved it, particularly as the price rose.

It didn't take long before people inside and outside the company knew of Suzuki and his successful pet project, which had afforded him a chance to satisfy his writing urges, but also made him something of an entrepreneur. A few years later, that latter designation would prove to be his calling.

Start by Fulfilling a Need

In the early 1970s, who would have thought that the arrival of a tiny retail store would set off a revolution in consumer purchasing habits and reshape both the retail and distribution sectors of Japan? It had the right hook. The stores were open 24 hours, and with a workforce fully accustomed to late nights at the office or blowing off steam until the wee hours of the morning, this was an idea ready for acceptance. Before long, there were 7-Eleven stores in every part of the country. The franchise has never looked back, continuing to outpace and outdistance its competition, which makes the story of how it came to be all the more compelling.

Store openings for 7-Eleven were carried out and operated as a subsidiary of mega Japanese supermarket chain, Ito-Yokado (now an equal constituent with 7-Eleven in Seven & i Holdings). A period dubbed by industry analysts as a "distribution renaissance in Japan" was so called because two retail giants, The Daiei, Inc., under its charismatic founder, Isao Nakauchi, and Ito-Yokado, under the equally magnetic Masatoshi Ito, were slugging it out for market share and retail hegemony. Price slashing had been Daiei's modus operandi since its inception in 1957, and Nakauchi, once quoted as saying his company sold everything except ladies and opium, had built his company into a high-volume, low-price retail giant for the masses, in direct confrontation with local commercial associations that existed in every community and banded together to set prices and business hours.

Often when Ito-Yokado (and Daiei) considered an outlet in a community, the local commercial associations would rise up against them, or at least try to hammer out some sort of co-existence deal that could benefit both parties.

For Ito-Yokado, which was carrying out an expansion drive called "area dominance strategy," a positive presence in these communities was viewed as a key to its business model success.

"We racked our brains trying to come up with a path that would lead to a happy co-existence," recalls Suzuki when he was still a part of Ito-Yokado management. "This dealt with people's livelihoods, so we all took it very seriously. That's when I heard of the convenience store concept of 7-Eleven in the US. By this time, we were desperate for a solution, so I decided to set off on a fact-finding tour."

But Suzuki upon his arrival in the US was in for a surprise:

> The information I had received before the trip was that this was a no-nonsense company that had some 4,000 franchise outlets to its credit already. I was eager to see what they had. But what I saw quite honestly didn't impress me. Quite the opposite, in fact.

Suzuki found the atmosphere in the stores to be somewhat dusky and uninviting, and product selection was poor. Not compelled to buy a single item in the stores, Suzuki questioned whether such an idea could succeed in Japan. His colleagues with him concurred.

Though far from convinced that this business model would arm them with anything useful for when they returned home, Suzuki and his team nevertheless went ahead with their original plans to take part in a convenience store management training program. By the third day, Suzuki had formulated an assessment:

> That convenience store format may prove ample and sufficient in the US market, but if Japanese like ourselves are going to use them, we're going to have to customize them accordingly.

While proceeding to analyze social conditions in America and the role of the convenience store in great detail, Suzuki began thinking of ways the model would have to be modified if brought to Japan. The first place he looked was in the area of food. The frozen sandwiches of American 7-Eleven stores may be the accepted and even preferred norm, but they didn't sit well with Suzuki:

> Whenever I looked at a frozen hamburger, I have to say it seemed very unappetizing. Nobody is going to put down good money for something that isn't appetizing. The 7-Eleven concept of America, quite frankly, would not meet the Japanese consumer expectations, and so I found little to be attracted by it.

Suzuki and company did learn what they could about the basic framework for operating a convenience store chain, but when it came to actual products and services, they would need to defer to their own ideas and demographic research. Thorough market research would become a key element to Suzuki's patented business style.

Scrupulous attention to the varying conditions of people and place would produce enormous results for Suzuki's venture. The strength of 7-Eleven in Japan can largely be attributed to its high return on assets, and perhaps equally to its high rate of growth. The strategy was never to squeeze the most mileage possible from a revolutionary commercial concept, but instead to establish a valuable new asset and fixture in consumers' lives.

For this reason, Suzuki was eager to move aggressively ahead of other companies to introduce the POS system in all 7-Eleven stores, for sales and inventory tracking. This would give him an accurate and real-time "snapshot" into consumption habits all across the country; precisely what he viewed as the key to transplanting the convenience store idea successfully in Japan.

One real difference between the US and Japanese system lay in how one counted up customer traffic. Do you base your business model on how many customers you brought into the store? Or how many customers you brought through the cash register? With POS, Suzuki chose the latter.

Be a Humble Pupil First. Then Get Creative

As mentioned earlier, Toshifumi Suzuki didn't take long after joining Ito-Yokado in 1962 to capture the attention of Masatoshi

Ito. He exhibited a passion for his work and had reams of energy. Nine years into his career at Ito-Yokado, when he was tapped to go to the US and accumulate management know-how for running a convenience store, he knew he had to pay close attention to what was being taught. But rather than learning to repeat the method, he quickly realized he only really needed to learn *from* it.

This resulted in an occasional disagreement with colleagues who had joined him on the mission:

> "What you're thinking runs completely counter to everything we learned!" they'd say to me. But I don't blame them. I mean, here we'd gone to the trouble of learning what was deemed as the best know-how in what was the global capital of business, and I seemed intent on outright rejecting it. So from their perspective, it was natural for them to question why we went to America in the first place, and doubt whether it was necessary.

There was one more very important reason behind Suzuki's decision not to apply a lot of what he'd learned about the business abroad. And that was his belief that while it may be described as a "store of convenience," Japanese would more likely view it, or use it, as a pared-down version of a supermarket or local store in their community; one that also happens to be open 24 hours.

The store may be smaller than a supermarket and carry a smaller assortment of goods, but Suzuki believed that a customer's reasons for entering the store would have to be viewed as generally the same reasons for patronizing a supermarket: to buy daily necessities, food and consumable goods such as batteries or toilet paper. The 7-Eleven stores Suzuki had seen in the US fell far short in terms of providing essential goods that he felt Japanese shoppers would be looking to buy. "If you aren't meeting customer needs," he would say, "the whole justification for bringing the business to Japan in the first place crumbles."

Thus Suzuki's mantra: "Don't simply imitate," which is followed by axioms of seeking to question everything, and to turn the task of making improvements into a daily, trial-and-error process.

Suzuki's take on the changes that would be required proved very astute. The items that lined the shelves reflected Japanese consumer tastes, particularly when seeing the rice balls, the box lunches, and ready-made meals of fresh—not frozen—ingredients that were on display on refrigerated shelves. These could be bought at any time of the day or night, which helped differentiate 7-Eleven from super-markets, as was the intention, and elevated brand awareness. What Suzuki created became truly something "convenient" and wel-comed by the Japanese consumer.

Ironically, it would be Suzuki several years later in 1991 who would bring Southland Corporation (now 7-Eleven, Inc.) under his management as a subsidiary of Ito-yokado and 7-Eleven Japan. This was the very American company from which he had received know-how and training, and sought initially to model his business after. It was a fabled case of pupil exceeding the master. At the time, Southland Corporation was experiencing dire financial woes and a management crisis. That eventually led to the rescuing and revamp-ing all of Southland Corporation's business, and returning it to prof-itability within three years. In the US, 7-Eleven is growing again, and worldwide it is the largest chain store in any category. Perhaps these achievements, more than any other, are what have brought Suzuki global attention as a world-class business leader.

Don't Be Hampered by Success

As keys to future business growth, Toshifumi Suzuki often warns of the dangers of becoming prisoner to one's past successes, along with extolling the virtues of constantly trying new things:

> 7-Eleven in the US ran into difficulty because at one point it stopped questioning its model, and began relying on past precedents of success. But you must always harbor doubts about whether what you're doing is right or not, whether you're on the right path for the future.

Certainly, there are many lessons to be learned and retained from past successes. The wisdom of those who have gone before exist in many timeless maxims and epithets that still ring true, and they can often provide great insight, courage, and inspiration for the future.

But most of these teachings are not etched in stone. They are not absolutes, but are didactic accounts of past successes and failures. One must appreciate their wisdom and value, but then reflect upon their relevance and meaning today and in one's own contextual setting. Otherwise, one might find oneself attempting the impossible. Suzuki reminds his people to look closely and carefully at those around them and the environment in which they live and work; study them, and clarify what needs to be done, and to what end. Above all, find the particular needs and wants in those places where one wishes to succeed. There's no point in fishing where there aren't any fish.

Learn to Read "Change"

"Single-item management" is a term coined by Toshifumi Suzuki. It means essentially to understand on an item-by-item basis what is selling and what is "dying" in order to raise precision in procurement. Suzuki aggressively introduced the POS system so that he could instantly see and consign to a database what was selling right at that moment directly from the cash register: information that plays a very critical role in determining purchasing behavior and trends.

At the core of Suzuki's philosophy is to strive for the ideal of offering precisely what the customer needs or wants at the moment it is wanted, rather than trying to *shape* the customer's needs and wants. This has been described as the "hospitality method," in other words, serving the customer like a guest in your home or at an inn. Japanese have for centuries been a people fond of—if not often consumed with—hospitality practices. To guarantee that a customer spends time in your store in the greatest comfort, you need to know his or her interests, tastes, and preferences in advance, and be ready to fulfill them. Knowing what will please the customer and providing it is the only way to ensure a successful and, perhaps, a return visit.

Suzuki believes that combining traditional elements, namely, a distinctly Japanese fascination with hospitality, with the right modern management tools can create the world's greatest convenience store chain.

Summary: Trust Built on Self-Merit

Seven & i Holdings is a general retail business that in fiscal 2008 recorded its highest annual revenues ever—six trillion yen—amid a troubled year for Japan's retail industry. At the core of this achievement is a business philosophy created and disseminated by Honorary Chairman Masatoshi Ito. Dubbed Ito's "Way of the Merchant," it is a stance that emphasizes the holding of high principles and vision, yet posited in a grounded, sincere, and honest way of life.

It is revealed in the accumulation of credibility and reliability among customers, and in a sense of humility that "companies do fail" and the customer is always right. It is executed through the selection of the best and most capable people who can help steer through the "riptides of change" and ensure a company's prosperity through future generations.

Masatoshi Ito was born in 1924, and at the age of five experienced the harrowing effects of the Great Depression, remembering how a carton of eggs sold at the family store would barely earn enough to cover the cost of the carton:

> We ran a small-to-medium-sized business where the loss of a single customer would mean not being able to pay an employee's salary. So we always rejoiced more at receiving compliments from an employee than at seeing the company grow. Credibility is something you accumulate from each individual customer and associate. Once you lose a sense of gratitude for that, your business is finished. Humility is most important.

Masatoshi Ito would go on to build one of the largest retail chains of all time in his Ito-Yokado superstores and affiliated holdings, and in the process become one of the world's richest men. But he remained ever humble and appreciative of others for his company's success, a trait that enabled him to choose and encourage great talent around him.

One of those Ito scouted early on was Toshifumi Suzuki, introduced to him through a mutual acquaintance. Suzuki was already 30 and had been working in a different industry, but Ito immediately sensed great potential and hired him. That was 1962. And within a mere eight years, Suzuki had risen to an executive management position at Ito-Yokado. As an outsider initially, Suzuki brought a relatively unprejudiced perspective toward the retail business, and took great interest in finding new ways to shore up what he saw as low productivity and inefficiencies among small-to-medium-sized retail shops.

But Suzuki got his chance to build a business from the bottom up with the launch of 7-Eleven in Japan in 1973 (then called York Seven Inc.). He didn't want to squander it by starting out with a business model that struck him as fraught with encumbrances. He intended from Day One to reshape the 7-Eleven format into something that would take root in Japanese soil and eventually yield a wholly new and independent culture around the "convenience store" idea.

"You can't be number one through imitation," Suzuki would say. "You have to stand ready to challenge conventional wisdom."

But doing so successfully involved the steady and meticulous accretion of credibility, something that is at the heart of Masatoshi Ito's business philosophy, and an important value in Japanese society overall. In a brand new market segment, trust would need to be built on one's own merit:

> If we were to stop seeking new challenges, we would find ourselves embroiled in a "war over volume," and decay would set in. Growth is predicated upon repeated reform and innovation carried out from the customer's perspective, and under a constant state of crisis that you may be falling behind the pace of change.

Suzuki cut his business teeth at the clothing and grocery superstore chain, Ito-Yokado, which fathered the 7-Eleven venture in Japan. Consumer spending was high in the booming economy of Japan in the 1970s, and Ito-Yokado was diversifying into restaurant operation that brought the Denny's family restaurant chain to Japan in 1973. Denny's Japan Co. continues to run more than 500 restaurants as a principal subsidiary of Seven & i Holdings.

But it was really the opening of the first 7-Eleven convenience store the next year that catapulted the Ito-Yokado group on a rapid growth trajectory. The Suzuki-led project threatened to revolutionize the Japanese distribution industry as the franchise business grew at a pace of 100 stores a year.

At the core of this heady expansion was a firm belief of Suzuki's that one must think with the mind of the "buyer," not the "seller," and that any new endeavors, groundbreaking or not, must ultimately be done in the name of satisfying the end user's needs. Once you can do that, it becomes much easier to discard ideologies and practices that were successful in the past, but may have little bearing on success in the future. As a caveat, however, Suzuki warns against resorting to mimicry and imitation of what others may be doing:

> In this ever-changing world, you must carry a sense of urgency about you at all times that you need to embrace new ideas and break with the past to grow your business. Otherwise, you will be assuredly left behind.

A sense of crisis, or urgency perhaps, courses through the veins of Suzuki's Seven & i Holdings. Things are always on the move. The belief is that constant improvements and modest successes here and there do accumulate over time to form the competitive muscle tissue of a company overall.

There has long been a tradition in Japan of treating the paying customer as always right manifesting itself in such a degree of deference and humility that bowing one's head and avoiding eye contact is seen as the way to win the customer's trust. But here, Suzuki, breaks with tradition in seeking to earn that trust more by responding to the customer's particular needs over time. Treating all customers equally and as always right, is not as effective a means for earning their trust as meeting their needs as "individuals."

For example, 7-Eleven stores paved the way in offering a wide variety of products and services that people needed at all hours of the day and night, such as 24-hour ATM banking, postal and parcel services, and transportation and entertainment ticketing. In fact, banking has now become Seven & i Holdings' second biggest profit maker following the convenience store business due to ATM fees. While other convenience store chains have followed suit, 7-Eleven's ability to attract customers is palpably stronger because of its high sensitivity to granular needs. The group didn't just set up ATMs as satellite services for existing banks, but entered full force into the banking industry in May 2001 by establishing the IY Bank, offering lower fees than banks and longer hours, not to mention giving customers access to an expansive network of ATMs that dwarfed the numbers banks provided. This level of commitment to serving changing customer needs is borne out by a higher per capita amount spent at 7-Elevens than at competing chains; a product of, as Suzuki intended, greater customer trust.

This kind of trust breeds brand loyalty and strengthens brand equity. Before launching a new product or service, Suzuki first asks whether it will serve an important need and thus strengthen customer loyalty to the brand. He then proceeds to balance the assessment of earnings the new offering is expected to generate with an assessment of predicted customer satisfaction. Too much of one without the other would be fruitless.

7-Eleven was the first retail business in Japan to aggressively implement and successfully introduce POS system cash registers, which allowed back-office management and distribution to know precisely what products were being sold where and at precisely what time.

While this was dubbed "single-product management," it was also "customer management" in that it provided real-time information about customer purchasing patterns and behavior.

Japanese consumers may be among the most finicky in the world. They are sticklers for detail and extremely sensitive to both service and product quality. The tiniest defect will prevent them from making a purchase, and suppliers are therefore quick to discard or discount items that might very well sell at retail prices elsewhere. But with the ever-increasing diversity of products and choices consumers have along with greater competition in the retail sector, there is only so much merchandise one 7-Eleven store can stock at one time. That is where brand strength and customer trust become so critically important.

Seven & i Holdings is recording record sales and profits amid one of the worst recessions in memory. As the 15th largest retailer in the world, it is expanding operations of its 35,000 convenience stores, supermarkets, superstores, department stores, restaurants and other concerns globally, and boosting presence in China under its area dominance strategy. But this is not about a good system on auto-pilot. If you look closely at the inner workings behind the scenes, you will see a company that is constantly monitoring, tweaking and innovating its business in a daily effort to build customer trust.

In a way, 7-Eleven is lucky to be in a business that affords such close daily contact with the consumer—within walking distance to nearly everyone in the country. As the chapter's title states, all that is needed for a good product to sell is to have a good place at which to sell it. But that, perhaps, is the easy part. Convenience stores are not a sure thing. They fail often. Success therefore lies in the definition of a "good place." For Toshifumi Suzuki, it is where you can earn the trust of customers on a daily basis, and continue earning that trust through a willingness to listen, and adapt.

Principal Ideas of Toshifumi Suzuki

- Never rest on your laurels. or experience of past success.
- You can't become number one by imitation.
- Always possess a sense of crisis and remove obstacles directly in front of you, one at a time.

Seven & i Holdings Co., Ltd.

Established: September 1, 2005
Toshifumi Suzuki, Chairman and CEO
Head office: 8–8, Nibancho, Chiyoda-ku, Tokyo
http://www.7andi.com/en/
Capital: 50,000 million yen (year ending February 2009)
Consolidated sales: 5, 649,948 million yen
Consolidated operating profit: 281,865 million yen
Consolidated net profit: 92,336 million yen
Group employees: 141,831

3

IS SOMETHING HOLDING
YOU BACK?

_____

Shinzo Maeda
President and CEO
Shiseido Co., Ltd.

Born February 1947 in Osaka. Graduated from the Faculty of Letters,
B.A. in Sociology of Keio University in 1970, then joined Shiseido.
Served as general manager of Cosmetics Strategic Planning Department,
Cosmetics Marketing Division, chief officer of the Asia–Pacific Regional
Headquarters, International Operations Division. Appointed president
and CEO in June 2005.

From Hair Growth Tonic and Toothpaste

When Arinobu Fukuhara, founder of Shiseido, opened Apothe-
cary Shiseido in Tokyo's fashionable Ginza district in 1872,
the country's first Western-style pharmacy was born. Fukuhara had
been a chief pharmacist to the Japanese Navy and, as a man of science, was disgruntled at the quality of Japanese medicine, setting
up Shiseido with the aim of separating its medical and dispensary
practices.

The Shiseido company name is derived from a passage in the classic
Chinese cosmological text, the *Yi Jing*, praising the virtues of the
Earth, which nurtures new life and brings forth significant values. By
also going with a Japanese camellia flower called *hanatsubaki* as the
company trademark, Shinzo Fukuhara, Arinobu's third son and an
accomplished photographer, drew plenty of symbolic inspiration from
Eastern tradition. But his business style would be patently Western.

Manufacturing, marketing, and selling advanced pharmaceutical products at a premium quality and price was how Shiseido aimed to build credentials and earn consumer trust. For example, the company introduced Japan's first toothpaste in 1888, which was much smoother than the salt and powdered limestone with which people had previously cleaned—and damaged—their teeth. While ordinary tooth powder was only minimally scented to hide its poor quality, Fukuhara Sanitary Toothpaste was scientifically designed to dissolve tartar and eliminate bad breath, making it not only a status symbol at many multiples the price of tooth powder, but a scientific advancement as well. The toothpaste was an instant hit that set the tone for Shiseido as an upscale brand with great cultural cachet, as evidenced by the name making it into a classic Natsume Soseki novel of the time, *Mon* (1910):

> He recalled how a law student in his dormitory would often stop in at Shiseido while out on a walk and nonchalantly spend close to five yen on a three-pack of soap and toothpaste. So what reason was there, he felt that he alone should fall into such destitution.

The Shiseido toothpaste mentioned in *Mon* cost one quarter of a yen, 25 *sen*, while a bag of other toothpastes on the market sold for between two and three *sen*. To get a better perspective, 25 *sen* at the time could get a person 12 miles across town by train over bad roads that would take half a day to cover on foot. This image as a coveted domestic brand would help pave the way for Shiseido's entry into the cosmetics business.

This entry would be based on the same principles that had scored the company great success in pharmaceuticals: high quality, spirit of innovation, and uncompromising authenticity. In 1897, Shiseido introduced a ruby red softening lotion with a Western name, Eudermine (lit. "good skin"), and sold it in a beautiful nouveau bottle worthy of high-class perfume or wine. Over a century later, evolving in tandem with Shiseido as Japan's premier cosmetics brand, Eudermine remains a favorite product today.

Early on, Arinobu Fukuhara was looking for interesting ways to expand his business, and set off on a fact-finding tour of the US and Europe in 1900. What he witnessed at American drugstores excited him, and provided him with new inspiration for his business back home. By 1902, using machines he had modeled after those seen in the US, Fukuhara introduced Japan's first soda fountain.

Nobody had seen anything like it before. Long lines of refreshments seekers formed around the Shiseido pharmacy after offering the soda fountain, a business that would grow into the Shiseido Parlour chain of upscale restaurants and food business today. Indeed, Shiseido is credited for popularizing sodas and ice-cream in Japan.

The spirit that Shiseido exhibited from its founding was of a maker and vendor of essential products for daily life that, while synonymous with luxury, sought to earn profound consumer loyalty and confidence through uncompromising authenticity. It is a spirit that continues to be passed through the company to this day.

Japanese Technology Travels

The cosmetics industry has historically been dominated by Western brands. Japanese cosmetics makers, even with all their technological savvy, have yet to leave their mark on the global complexion.

While there are several possible explanations for this— discrepancies in skin types and tones between Asians and Westerners; culturally based differences as to the kinds of makeup and skin care that should be applied—the fact remains that it is very difficult for Japanese cosmetics makers to muscle in on the strong mindshare that Western cosmetics brands command. People's attitudes and opinions toward cosmetics brands are frequently set even before visiting a makeup counter and testing a product. Many customers remain deeply loyal to a select few brands or products with which they have found past success, so the barrier for new entrants is extremely high.

Shiseido is no fledgling, however. The company has been producing and selling cosmetics for 136 years, long enough to build up a legitimately strong profile in Western countries as a high-quality, luxury brand; precisely the image Arinobu Fukuhara had in mind when he opened his first pharmacy in Ginza over a century ago. While Shiseido has commanded near monolithic support and trust from consumers domestically, it has had to battle for every inch of market position abroad.

"There is no reason our products shouldn't be enjoying a better reputation and stronger growth abroad," proclaimed one Shiseido executive dissatisfied with the company's reliance on domestic demand when its brand image seems so strong abroad.

That executive was Shinzo Maeda, a 37-year company veteran who upon becoming Shiseido president and CEO in 2005 decided to preserve the Shiseido traditions while remaking the brand and carrying out the most sweeping reforms the company had seen in a hundred years.

Breaking with the Past, However Glorious

Shinzo Maeda shocked a lot of people when he started taking the axe to legacy brands and products Shiseido had spent the past century building. To him, the company had grown unwieldy with too many product lines demanding too much attention and resources, and thereby diluting total brand strength and management efficiency. Maeda's strategy was to consolidate the number of product lines down to about one-fourth the number it had when he took office, and to do so without delay. The swiftness with which Maeda intended to revamp the company invariably led to deep consternation and even anger among various stakeholders, and some even expressed in hushed tones misgivings about his sanity.

But Maeda's reply was adamant. "If we're going to reform the company for the twenty-first century, then now is the time." He stressed that failure to take bold measures now would only kick the can down the road, and lead to greater pain and losses in the future. What everyone could agree upon was that maintaining the status quo was not an option. Shiseido still owned a near 20 percent share of Japan's beauty industry and could boast strong earnings, but the market was saturated with an increasing number of local and foreign competitors, and Maeda was set on propelling the company toward its next "evolutionary stage."

Shiseido could certainly point to a glorious evolutionary history. But like many other long-surviving companies that had become so large and proud as to be nearly synonymous with the industries they led, the years and years of expansive growth at Shiseido had given birth to a multitude of sub-brands and product lines that were now beginning to weigh heavily on the corporate body in an era marked by shrinking demand and intensifying competition.

To be sure, a strong argument could have been made for keeping all the various brands and product lines. Each had their own loyal customer bases and undoubtedly held varying degrees of importance or value to Shiseido's earnings or image. Indeed, there had been a time when the number of product lines one could churn out did demonstrate a company's strength and staying power. But here Shiseido seemed to have gone overboard, often forgetting to articulate the true purpose behind these brands, or failing to reassess their value or positioning once launched. The age of unlimited expansion was over. A new set of goals tailored to new twenty-first-century realities were needed.

The Maeda reforms led to a reborn Shiseido under a clearer brand message and greater customer orientation that began with an exhortation to literally "stop all of the incessant doing and making." Shiseido had followed a traditional business style in most Japanese consumer product industries to release new product lines into the market regularly. But this nurtured a myopic emphasis on "novelty" and "freshness" at the cost of fortifying existing brands and nurturing them for the long term. Maeda's first imperative therefore was to "take the hand off the pump:"

> Having many brands is not a bad thing in and of itself. But breeding them became their own justification. We had to get back to basics and turn our attention to answering the all-important and obvious question of "What is a brand?" Having so many in our lineup also meant keeping a swollen inventory. While we could have lived with that in the past, we can't afford to do that anymore. So we had to start viewing that behavior as extravagant, as a function of faulty planning. In some respects, that meant taking a crowbar to 136 years of the Shiseido edifice, pulling up some of the old floorboards and rebuilding from scratch.

Needless to say, Maeda's decision struck many at Shiseido as audacious and even presumptuous. Yet they needed to get behind their leader, and move ahead with unified purpose if they were to succeed. So the work began to recast the brand in a completely different, and hopefully brighter, light.

The centerpiece of this brand renovation thus far has been represented by the introduction of two "mega lines" for the domestic market, called "Maquillage" and "Tsubaki" (Japanese camellia). Maquillage was positioned as a "total makeup brand," a full line of makeup and counseling-based products targeted at the 25-to-35-year-old age bracket. Maquillage was launched as a glamorous product line in 2005 under a motto that roughly translates as, "The Advent of the Beauty Climax."

Tsubaki, on the other hand, was fashioned into a hair care brand, and was positioned as the fourth "mega line" in the brand consolidation project. Tsubaki, Japanese for the camellia that adorns the Shiseido logo, aimed to offer products that re-establish the wondrous virtues of camellia japonica oil, long used to set hair in Japan.

When Tsubaki was launched in the spring of 2006, Shiseido had set a target of 10 billion yen in sales for the first year. It reached half that target within a month, and promptly rose to market share leadership.

"Not everything is going to prove successful, and each day brings new targets to shoot for," reflected Maeda. "So while the brand reform effort will be ongoing, we've already reduced the number of product lines from 100 to 27. The second three-year-plan we initiated in 2008 aims to narrow that number to 21. But we have to press on to ensure that our simultaneous 'distinction and concentration' effort takes root as the new modus operandi in our company."

Quality Trumps Quantity in Both Products and People

The recruitment and development of great people formed the third leg of the Maeda management vision initiated in 2005:

> It is meaningless to just have good products, because it takes people to handle them. People manage them, develop them, promote them, and ultimately sell them. So in every field of endeavor and in every aspect of the business, you need to foster talent. Otherwise, your products, as good as they may be, will never find themselves in the hands of the end user. For that purpose, we decided to do away with an emphasis on numerical indicators for evaluating performance. Instead, we have become thoroughly focused on the pursuit of quality over quantity. For example, we've discarded a style of customer interaction that is focused on simply selling products, and opted for one that instead encourages customers to come in for consultations as often as they wish to build a relationship of trust.

Cultivating people who can earn the implicit trust of the customer is what Maeda believes will ultimately elevate Shiseido's brand value. His first three-year plan eliminated sales quotas for beauty consultants. As of the first half of 2008, more than 80 percent of Shiseido sales were credited to 27 newly consolidated product lines with the six "mega lines" accounting for more than 40 percent.

Respond to Changing Circumstances and Diversity of Demand

Even before markets around the world found themselves roiled by a deepening recession starting in the fall of 2008, the captains of Japanese industry had become painfully aware that they could no longer stake their companies' survival on domestic demand. While exports had driven the growth of the automobile and consumer electronics sectors for years, the importance of the global market-place had grown to encompass most other business sectors as well, particularly in Japan, where the population was and remains on the decline.

Shiseido has always been eager to look overseas for organic growth, and was the first among its domestic competitors to reposition itself as a company with global intentions, starting most notably in Asia. Shinzo Maeda's road map for the decade beginning with the second three-year plan in 2008 is bullish about Shiseido's prospects there:

> We set a sales target of a trillion yen by 2018, and half of that we project will come from overseas. In the past few years, aided by the excitement generated by the Beijing Olympics, we grew at a rate of 30 percent or higher between 2005 and 2008 in China. Just as we did in Japan, we have high hopes for building a broader customer base by deploying our products through specialty Perfumerie networks. Other Japanese cosmetics makers have since followed suit, hoping to use China as a launching pad for fanning out across Asia. So we have to make sure we can leverage the gains we accrued by our earlier arrival, and continue growing as a company with the highest consumer trust and mindshare in those markets.

Shiseido followed its China initiative with a move into urban centers across Asia and in Russia to harness the strong brand equity that already exists as a luxury cosmetics brand. In this sense, Shiseido remains committed to the well-heeled image its products have always boasted, even as it looks to provide more affordable price points for its products in China that still live up to a premium standard.

Beginning in 2008, amid the severe global economic downturn, Shiseido decided to debut its overseas cosmetics under a single name: Shiseido, the company name, to serve as an easily identifiable flagship brand. This is becoming something of an astute global marketing move among Japanese companies that have conventionally managed multiple brands, such as Matsushita Electric Industrial Co., which recently consolidated under the Panasonic moniker.

Shiseido products are slated for sale in more than 70 countries worldwide. Among them is a high-end skin care product that retails for more than $300, part of a product amplification strategy intended to position luxury cosmetics as a cornerstone of Shiseido's overseas operations in 2009. But in these trying economic times, will high-end cosmetics sell?

"Time will tell," says Maeda. "But over the next five years, our objective is to turn Shiseido into a billion-dollar brand in annual sales."

Shiseido's target audience is quite clear—trend-sensitive women in their 30s and 40s who will gravitate toward the luxury line's emphasis on both luxury and natural beauty, with all products emphasizing their plant-based ingredients and the gentleness of nature in maintaining healthy skin.

Don't Wait for a Crisis to Force Change

"We had reached a point where all we were really doing was churning out products and seeing how much mileage we could get from them," laments Maeda about Shiseido before 2005. "So I went around to various vendors to meet directly with our beauty consultants, and told them to clear their minds of numbers. I asked them to, instead, devote their mental energies to thinking of how to make their customers more beautiful."

Maeda made extensive *genba* shopfloor rounds armed with some new motivational priorities for his sales force, and to relieve them of the pressure to sell that didn't seem to be doing the consultants, the customers, or the brand much good.

It has become a mantra in business administration texts to view crisis as a prime opportunity for radical change. But even a dire need for change still requires a strong mental fortitude and conviction at the top of an organization. When Carlos Ghosn was sent by French automaker, Renault, to restructure its partner and ailing auto giant, Nissan Motors, in 1999, there was a sense that only an "outsider" could execute the radical changes that the company needed. A Japanese manager would face too much internal hostility, and would buckle under the immense pressure of precedent and calcified loyalties. Ghosn did turn Nissan around, succeeding where no Japanese manager could have at the time, and creating a model for action that others could and would emulate, if they so dared.

One company man who must have been paying close attention to the dramatic turnaround orchestrated at Nissan in the late 1990s was Shinzo Maeda. When he became president and CEO of Shiseido, Maeda displayed a remarkable strength of will and foresight to undertake the task of streamlining a giant creaking ship in advance of a global recession that still lay unseen on the distant horizon. What's more, he displayed an "audacity" to tamper with the glorious legacy of his company's past.

Maeda waxes hopeful at the relative advantage his company has over rivals to make inroads into new markets, and reposition Shiseido as a global player in a sector long dominated by Western brands. It is all owing to a forward-looking process of business restructuring that began some five years ago.

Summary: Unwavering Tradition and Tireless Innovation

By the time Arinobu Fukuhara opened Japan's first Western-style pharmacy, Shiseido, in Tokyo's Ginza district in 1872, he already knew a lot about his trade. His grandfather had been a doctor of Oriental medicine, and Fukuhara himself a chief pharmacist at a navy hospital. But Fukuhara had a slightly different vocational direction in mind when Shiseido began manufacturing and selling skin care products in 1897, and laying the foundation for what would become Japan's cosmetics giant, the Shiseido Company.

"Foreign imports and Western goods were all the rage at the time, but when it came to cosmetics, Japan was still locked in the Edo Period," wrote Fukuhara. "I wanted to take advantage of all the advances being made in contemporary pharmaceutical sciences to come up with homegrown products more tailored to the physiology and tastes of Japanese women."

Fukuhara's high regard for Western culture and science was reinforced when he visited the US and Europe, including a stopover at the 1900 World Expo in Paris. Upon his return, he began producing a slew of products from vitamins to toothpaste, and was even instrumental in the establishment of the government-initiated Dai-Nippon Pharma Company. He eventually left the management of Shiseido to his third son, Shinzo, who studied cosmetics and fashion in the US and France before returning home to help transform the company's core business from drugstore products to cosmetics. Designing the *hanatsubaki* (camellia flower) trademark himself, Shinzo worked hard to build a unique aesthetic culture around the brand, employing top designers and supporting the arts. The Shiseido Gallery was opened in 1919. Shinzo invited Noboru Matsumoto as a business strategist. Matsumoto had studied marketing at New York University, and he became Shiseido's second president.

In 1921, Shiseido established Shiseido's Five Principles of Quality First, Co-existence, Co-prosperity, Respect for Customers, Corporate Stability through a firm foundation with long-range goals, and Sincerity. In 1923, second president Matsumoto then set about building the first nationwide, voluntary cosmetics chain store system, which served to link manufacturer, distributor, retailer, and consumer together in a symbiotic relationship where each stakeholder could expect reasonable profits thanks to a uniform pricing system. As the number of contracted retail stores swelled to the thousands, a unique Shiseido culture took root, associated with quality, modernity, and Western aesthetics.

Shiseido flourished for the next 140 years as Japan's flagship cosmetics maker, but has embarked on the twenty-first century with a second three-year plan to become a leading global player. The man who has eagerly taken up that mission since 2005 is Shinzo Maeda, who is intent on not only expanding the business internationally, but also rebuilding the company's brand strategy from the bottom up.

While Shiseido has sold products overseas since the 1950s, it found market conditions and demands quite different from those in Japan. It became clear that in advanced Western markets, they couldn't go it alone. Shiseido formed a joint venture in 1980 with medium-sized French cosmetics company, Pierre Fabre, hiring local branding experts after having rolled out a high-end makeup line called "Moisture Mist" in 1978. Shiseido then switched into higher gear in 1989 with the launch of a full range of cosmetic products called simply, "Shiseido—Makeup." But the first place the new global initiative really began to gain traction was China.

Shiseido had already been actively importing and selling cosmetics to foreign expatriates in China, but from 1983 began sharing technology with state-owned cosmetics makers, starting with shampoo and rinse products, and gradually expanding to hand lotions and cosmetics products. All of these were shipped and sold under Chinese brand names. This continued for a little more than 10 years before Shiseido sealed a partnership with the capital city of Beijing in 1991 to sell in high-end department stores a brand designed exclusively for the Chinese market, called "Aupres."

Support for the product spread quickly, making Aupres the number one-selling luxury cosmetic brand in most department stores. Shiseido's overseas share of total sales grew rapidly, rising to nearly 40 percent by the end of 2008. The company's "10-Year Roadmap" objective now is to split its earnings ratios evenly between foreign and domestic sales.

In branding itself at home and increasingly abroad as a top-of-the-line cosmetics maker, Shiseido owes much of its success to a comprehensive marketing strategy rooted in values the company has cherished since its founding: providing people with high-quality products, promoting a culture of health and beauty, and patiently building enduring relationships of trust with customers over time.

This is evident in the primary vision that Maeda articulated in his three-year plans for Shiseido to "become a 100-percent customer-oriented company," removing sales quotas and other obstacles that had impeded a sense of unity with customers. This is also the driving principle behind the steady brick-by-brick expansion strategy the company is carrying out in China that has led to the establishment of some 5,000 voluntary chain stores and the best-selling cosmetics brand in the world's fastest-growing market. To Maeda, a "customer orientation" means increasing points of contact with end users every-where. He has confidence that Shiseido's traditional values travel well; particularly its passion for excellence. If he is right, the center of grav-ity in the cosmetics world, like that of the global economy at large may, at last, shift East.

Principal Ideas of Shinzo Maeda

- A quality brand must travel worldwide.
- If you can grasp what customers seek and set clear goals, you are bound to succeed.
- Follow through on your aims with unfaltering resolve.

Shiseido Co., Ltd.

Established: June 24, 1927

Shinzo Maeda, President and CEO

Head office: 5-5, Ginza 7-chome, Chuo-ku, Tokyo

http://www.shiseido.co.jp/com/

Capital: 64,500 million yen (year ending March 2009)

Consolidated sales: 690,256 million yen

Consolidated operating profit: 49,914 million yen

Consolidated net profit: 19,373 million yen

Employees: 28,810

4

THE CUSTOMER ALWAYS TRUMPS LEGACY

Satoru Iwata
President and CEO
Nintendo Co., Ltd.

Born December 6, 1959 in Hokkaido, Japan. Satoru Iwata worked part time selling computers in a department store soon after graduating from the Computer Science faculty of Tokyo Institute of Technology's Engineering Department. Together with some fellow workers, he established a software development company called HAL Laboratory, Inc., where they began providing software primarily to Nintendo. In 2000, Iwata moved to Nintendo and was made chief of the Corporate Planning Division, from where he was tapped on June 1, 2002 to take over as president and CEO. In a company where the past three successive presidents had come from the founding Yamauchi family, Iwata seemed to come out of nowhere, surprisingly climbing over the company's elder oligarchs to the presidency.

Nintendo: Humble Beginnings as a Playing Card Company

The company that was established in Kyoto in 1889 was originally called Nintendo Koppai and founded by Fusajiro Yamauchi to produce a hand-drawn traditional Japanese card game called *Hanafuda*. Because the game involves a lot of fast hand action snapping up cards, the rapid wear-and-tear they underwent led to a constant stream of orders, making it a long-selling hit product for the company.

In 1902, Nintendo became the first Japanese company to produce Western-style playing cards. When it started manufacturing mahjong tiles, Nintendo's image and fame grew as a game and toy company.

When Fusajiro Yamauchi failed to produce a son with his wife, he handed the reins to the company over to his daughter's husband, who took on the name Yamauchi. It was his son, Fusajiro's grandson, Hiroshi Yamauchi, who would take Nintendo to soaring heights as an electronic game company. But Hiroshi showed a flair for business early, making aggressive moves such as negotiating the rights to use Disney characters on his playing cards to push sales. Under his stewardship, Nintendo would rise to blue-chip company status and be listed on the Tokyo Stock Exchange's First Section, where all of Japan Inc.'s heavyweights were traded.

The name "Nintendo" got its name from the Chinese characters "submit" and "heaven," signifying that a lot of life must be left to chance, or fate. In other words, do all that is humanly possible and let God take care of the rest. It is a spirit that courses through the veins of Nintendo to this day: a belief in not hurrying results but instead steadily accumulating them through daily hard work and dedication.

Not until the mid-1970s did Hiroshi Yamauchi, after seeking success in a variety of fields, began to steer the company in the direction of a budding arcade and home videogame market. The company scored relative hits with early infrared light-based, videogame consoles hooked up to televisions. But it wasn't until the first couple of years of the 1980s with the breakout arcade game, *Donkey Kong*, and the launch of a revolutionary handheld game device called Game & Watch that Nintendo began to earn large profits and demonstrate market leadership. Fitting into the palm of one's hand and boasting a revolutionary liquid crystal display, Game & Watch has come to be considered the forerunner to the Nintendo DS that dominates the handheld game console market today.

But it would be 1983 that would prove the breakout year for Nintendo with the debut of a product that would make its name synonymous with videogaming around the world: the Family Computer, "Famicom" for short in Japan. It was launched in the US a year later as the Nintendo Entertainment System, but came to be called simply "Nintendo." While there had been other television-connection game systems on the market, the Nintendo Family Computer offered users the convenience of switching in and out games with the use of game cartridges, but more significantly, Nintendo began licensing its platform to third-party game developers. It was a groundbreaking move that ultimately engendered the multibillion-dollar game industry that exists today.

Until then, toy manufacturers had made videogame consoles with all the games you could ever play on the system already included. Nintendo with its Family Computer system was essentially inviting anyone to build on it, thus opening up a whole new market and industry.

Personal computing was still in its nascency, but the debut of easy-to-use PCs such as the NEC PC8801 and MSX had spawned a new generation of young Japanese who were aspiring to become hit game or computer programmers, and they swarmed to the Family Computer platform.

Among them was a brilliant young programmer named Shigeru Miyamoto, a Nintendo employee whose game, *Super Mario Brothers* became a phenomenal hit among children and adults alike. It was the "killer app" that truly drove initial sales of the Family Computer hardware system. Incidentally, more than 40 million units of *Super Mario* were sold worldwide, and it remains one of the most popular games today, still available as an online download.

Nintendo Enters a New Age Under Satoru Iwata

Current Nintendo president, Satoru Iwata, is said to have loved electronics and computers so much that as a college student, he took a part-time job at a department store just so he could spend the day playing with them.

Iwata was a passionate and technically astute programmer. Together with other computerphile colleagues, Iwata started a game software venture called HAL Laboratory, Inc., where he quickly demonstrated that he was a man of extraordinary talent.

His timing was right, too. The Family Computer had just been released, and the world of home computer gaming had been blown wide open. Iwata set about programming games that would become instant classics for the Nintendo system, such as *Balloon Fight* and *Golf*, while setting new standards in graphics sophistication.

Iwata used elegant and simple-to-understand programming language that quickly elevated him to cult status among programmers and gamers both inside and outside of Japan. With his mounting fame and fortune, he found most of his workweeks soon being taken up by the day-to-day management of his company, to the point where he had to come in on weekends and holidays to satisfy his love for programming.

Because he was first and foremost a creator rather than a manager, Iwata has always had a shopfloor perspective. Rather than asking impertinent managerial questions, such as how to raise efficiency in the company, he is more likely to ask, "What can we make that will really wow the user?" Or "How can we program this more efficiently?"

To this day, Iwata will roll up his sleeves and spend hours working alongside employees. Or if a problem arises on the programming end, he's often one of the first on the scene talking and troubleshooting through the problem. Iwata is by nature and nurture a hands-on shopfloor manager, loath to leading by memo.

To make sufficient time for this, however, Iwata shuns media appearances as much as possible. He doesn't even appear at confabs that do not directly address software or programming issues. Though never too comfortable with a public persona, Iwata would gladly shrug off food and sleep to program, and believes that creating great games and wonderful new avenues for amusement is what speaks most to Nintendo's past, present, and future success above anything else.

Japan's Gaming Wars

Nintendo's ability to repeatedly revolutionize computer games—the Wii and DS gaming platforms being the most recent examples— has created something of a Midas touch aura to the company that its leaders would be quick to refute. For it hasn't all been smooth sailing, and the waters in this industry are always turbulent.

As a quick overview, the evolution of the home gaming console at Nintendo went thus: Family Computer (Nintendo Entertainment System), Super Family Computer (Super Nintendo Entertainment System), The Nintendo 64, The Nintendo Game Cube and the Wii. In handheld consoles, it went: Game Boy (first generation), Game Boy Pocket, Game Boy Light, Game Boy Color, Game Boy Advance, Game Boy Advance SP, Game Boy Micro, followed in succession by the Nintendo DS, DS Lite, and DSi.

But there is one device that is often missing from the list. It was called the Virtual Game Boy, and debuted simultaneously with the Nintendo 64 as a three-dimensional screen game device.

At the time, the landscape in videogaming was cluttered with a host of players all vying rigorously for coveted market share, and competing to see which among them was going to come out with the next revolutionary platform. Even Panasonic had entered the fray with its own gaming iteration.

Panasonic debuted what it dubbed the "3DO," using what was at the time groundbreaking imaging technology and large-data capacity through the use of CD-ROM. It was widely believed among industry watchers that the world was on the cusp of an age when everything with an electric plug could or would serve as its own multimedia platform. 3DO, too, was to be such a device.

Rivaling the Nintendo 64 in the Japanese market at the time were the Sony PlayStation, Sega's Sega Saturn, and NEC's Super CD-ROM². Outside Nintendo, these companies were all heavy hitters in the consumer electronics field globally, and they were focusing on superlative machine specifications to drive their sales appeal.

Concerned about falling behind, and hoping to offset any such disadvantage by demonstrating its technological might, Nintendo released the Virtual Game Boy. The device came in the shape of a large head-mounted display, where one had to peer into the device to play a game. With one's eyes fixed and fully occupied by the device, and no visual access to the outside world, the console concentrated solely on simulating a three-dimensional visual world. But its fatal flaw lay in the screen only being able to display images in red and black.

The Virtual Game Boy became synonymous with "user-unfriendliness." Though it had the name "Game Boy" attached to it, you couldn't really take it outside. That sealed its fate.

Meanwhile, Sony and Sega were capturing gamers' hearts and competitive edge with what at the time were called polygon graphics, technology originally developed by the US military involving combinations of computer-generated polygon shapes on a flat grid to make three-dimensional perspective images. (Nintendo had used similar image renderings in its games but most were essentially flat computer-dot graphics no different from the past.)

Sega, on the other hand, could distinguish itself by building on the sophisticated arcade games it had been deploying throughout the country's "game centers" (arcades) by coming out with pared down versions for home video consoles.

Sega was enjoying tremendous success with its polygon-based martial arts fighting game, *Virtua Fighter*, which drove competitive electronic gaming between two or more players to new heights in popularity and became a long-seller. While commercial arcade centers would have to shell out two million yen per unit, anyone who wanted unlimited play of the popular game could now get it on their Sega Saturn at home.

But the gap between the explosive popularity of certain amusement center games, and the hit-and-miss, four-year development cycle of home gaming devices grew larger. In short, being able to play to one's heart's content at home had been the main selling point of home consoles, but the level and quality of the game software being produced for them had become surprisingly low and ungratifying. Gradually, Nintendo users began to defect to Sega, leaving only a core of true believers.

Nintendo Sounds the Alarm for the Future

As it turns out, the sole winner to emerge from the home gaming wars where graphics mattered most was Sony. Nintendo remained viable because it did succeed in cornering the handheld game market with its Game Boy platform, despite the Virtual Game Boy fiasco. Nintendo proved adept at changing direction quickly and re-establishing priority on the portability of the Game Boy platform, and focused on boosting its functionality and features, while waiting for the next big opportunity to strike back in the home game space.

Sophisticated specs were not what Game Boy users sought. As a matter of fact, the Sega handheld counterpart, Game Gear, which boasted much greater sophistication and performance irked consumers because of short battery life. The color display consumed a lot of power. Plus it was too expensive a platform for both consumers and game developers. As a result, it died through natural selection.

Then something occurred that pulled Nintendo's coals from the fire. A game came out in 1996 that didn't initially gain very much traction but within months, through word of mouth mostly, was in such demand that a huge supply shortage ensued. The game was *Pocket Monsters*.

It has become the main driver of Game Boy device sales. Because *Pocket Monsters* was a huge TV, movie, and merchandising franchise, it allowed Nintendo to reap the added benefits of being part of a "media mix" strategy.

This was an epiphany for Nintendo. It wasn't about great graphics or processing speed, but simply about a great piece of software for the Game Boy. Nintendo took the opportunity to sound the alarm and remind the world and itself that it "should never again get caught up in a race for the biggest and best specs."

In a rare interview in 2007 with the *Nihon Keizai* newspaper, Iwata remarked:

> Even if someone were to come out right now with a game device with 10 times the machine performance as those on the market now, I wonder to what extent children would really notice the difference. It would be treading on dangerous ice to stake one's business model on targeting the fraction of game users who would know or care about the difference.

That this Game Boy software had become a nationwide hit had nothing to do with game specs. *Pocket Monsters* was a black-and-white dot image, low-spec game. Iwata was issuing something of a warning that the industry would crumble if it continued to ignore game content and focused on how much computing power a device had, how many cycles the CPU ran at, or how many calculations took place in the image processing.

Nintendo had grounds for making this claim.

They were looking back to the example of the sudden disappearance of an American game company called Atari that had risen to the top of the industry before 1982 and Nintendo's expansion overseas. In game circles, this was referred to as the "Atari shock."

Despite the growing sophistication of gaming specs at the time, the Atari shock exemplified a problem endemic in the computer game industry at the time: the quality of the content did not match the technical wizardry. It was a time when gamemakers believed anything would sell. But that wasn't the case. As makers stopped listening to consumers, consumers got bored. In that sense, parallels could be drawn to the situation today.

The focus on specs has led to video games boasting a high degree of visual realism or cinematic quality, proudly displaying the power of the technology, but often little else.

This kind of muscle gaming made large amounts of capital and technology indispensable among software makers, weeding out many third party developers who had great ideas but only modest tools and means to produce them.

Nintendo has, however, consistently positioned itself as a counterweight to a trend that is all about sophisticated graphics and speed.

The worldwide success of the Wii and DS platforms has thus far vindicated that stance. What earned these products immense support was, first, Nintendo got rid of the traditional game controller and the style of game play it dictated, and invented a way for whole families to play video games together. With easier, more intuitive controls, you didn't have to be an expert in a game to enjoy it.

As it turned out, Nintendo showed that most customers were, after all, not the kinds of users that placed much of a premium on game specs.

Being Revolutionary Means Doing Away with Past Legacy

In developing the Wii platform, Nintendo made the decision to break away from the standard game controller–with its "plus," A, and B buttons–that Nintendo itself had brought into the world and a format on which an entire industry had grown.

If you've ever played with a Sony PlayStation console, you may have wondered why the directional controls are laid out as they are; spaced relatively inconveniently apart. Going from up to down and left to right is like hopping on stepping stones.

The reason for this difficult layout is that Nintendo owns the patent on the plus button. It was a real groundbreaker in video game play to have a plus button that could easily be combined with the A and B buttons to facilitate play as well as to move freely between characters or players in a game screen. It is a big reason the Family Computer, as its name suggests, was so readily and well received by families, and laid the foundation for today's gargantuan computer game industry.

The controller as a game interface is paramount in importance as a bridge between the imaginary world inside the game, and reality. Yet with the Wii and DS, Nintendo completely threw it out.

By opting for a brand new technology using an infrared remote control "pointing device" for the Wii, and a screen-direct touch stylus for the DS, which had earned great user support thanks to the popularity of Sharp's personal digital assistant device, the Zaurus, Nintendo completely overhauled its game interface.

It probably wasn't an easy choice to do away with the iconic plus and A, B buttons standard, because it represented a valuable technological and cultural property as well.

Satoru Iwata, in another interview he gave to a game magazine, says that when developing the Wii and the DS, he received a pat of encouragement from Nintendo chairman Hiroshi Yamauchi.

"We have the constitution to endure one or two more failures in the hardware [game device] area. So proceed without fear and go make the best gaming experience you can."

Overcome by a sense of gratitude, Iwata says he shook Yamauchi's hand, and then set about on his first personal attempt at hardware development.

So what needs to be done to get the consumer to take up your game console? The proposition Iwata came up with was to abolish the controller and make game software more accessible to people. The simpler the rules to a game are, the easier it is to play. The rules to many card games, ball games, stone skipping, and jump rope are eminently simple, and anyone can learn to play after one simple explanation or demonstration.

To be sure, computer game rules had grown complex, presenting an increasingly formidable barrier to entry. Iwata was intent on rectifying that because if there's one thing you don't want to do, it is to keep out the general users that had opened up the gaming universe in the first place.

Nintendo's "gambit" paid off, creating a whole new genre of gaming and subsequently bringing a new user demographic into the fold by breaking with traditional computer game formats and subjects. Nothing has borne this out better than a software series for the DS designed to stimulate the brain, dubbed *DS Training for the Adult Brain*, which was an explosive hit, selling more than five million units.

This unconventional approach won the unmitigated support of veteran gamers, who acknowledged and welcomed a wholly new type of play. A common phenomenon for both DS and Wii game software thus far has been their sustained sales long after their release. Most hit software titles for these two platforms have become long-sellers.

When looking back over the history of game software development, most games accrue most of their total sales within the first three months of their release. Actually, the same has been said of book and CD sales. But the DS and Wii have overturned that commonly held notion.

One reason these games continue to sell might be the "games' universal value." Games to date have generally been built around the proposition of a start and a goal. Once you play the game through and reach its ending, there's little to get you to pick up that game a second time. In other words, the moment you reach the end of the game, the game's value immediately plunges. This happened because game developers began introducing storylines to their games, mass-producing computer games that were like movies or novels, and that became much the norm for the game development industry overall.

Many of the games that sell over the long term do not have endings programmed into them. There are, of course, objectives and targets to achieve, but they encourage the user to come back and try again; to do better the next time. Popular games across the board, not just on the DS or Wii, exhibit these traits.

An extra factor tied to earning the support of consumers has been the ease with which Nintendo products appeal to people of all ages and gender. Computer games have very rarely become topics of excitement and conversation among children *and* their parents. Most game content to date has been very enthusiast driven. Indeed, television commercials for the Wii feature families standing in their living rooms and playing computer games together, while the DS commercials often feature elderly celebrities, who don't fit the image of being computer game-savvy, enjoying themselves playing the games. Like the brain-training games for the DS (and now the Wii), the new remote game controller with its accelerometer technology turns the family game system also into a physical exercise device, an intended aim by Nintendo as seen with the release of the Wii Fit exercise board, which can gauge balance, pressure, and even act as a scale measuring weight and body fat. More than 15 million of the boards have been sold at last count.

Nintendo has worked hard to staunchly defend what has proven to be a consistent brand message since the company's founding a century ago. The playing card game, *Hanafuda*, that gave the company its start is traditionally played by the family during New Year's holidays, one of the few times that families get together. The use of the word "family" in Family Computer underscored that message because the device not only revolutionized home entertainment, but also did succeed in bringing its appeal to all members of the family, and all demographics, though not to the extent now that the Wii and DS are achieving. Nintendo has to the best extent possible kept extreme graphic violence and sexuality out of its software. Third-party developers have often been required to make changes to the levels of violence or blood shown in their games before they will be adopted on Nintendo platforms. In that sense, it's a bit of a shame that the word "Family" wasn't used overseas, because it does serve to communicate an essential message of the brand. The success of the Wii and

DS systems is testament to the benefits of staying the course in brand messaging, even while a company may overhaul or dismantle legacy products or services.

By keeping "family" in its sights, Nintendo has overturned the image of computer games as being at heart something exclusively for children, and instead sought to stimulate the child in everyone. That is why one of the first innovations Nintendo tackled with the Wii was to make the games expandable and playable by four people. This is great for business, too, because it can quadruple the number of computer game consumers in a household.

In keeping with the principles of Nintendo's founding Yamauchi family, Satoru Iwata has succeeded in taking what could very well have remained a niche market and given it massive global appeal, daring to reinvent things when necessary. Nintendo has grown into a major global company and industry leader by sticking to the philosophy and values that have served it best, but it has never been afraid to discard and redesign the format and expression those values take, and venture down new paths to success.

Not Winning or Losing, But Fulfilling One's Charter

Nintendo is however famous for not publicly stating its strategies. Apart from publishing its financials each year, it holds its cards closely to the chest, limiting announcements to new hardware releases at major industry venues, notably the Electronic Entertainment Expo (E3) held in California.

So it was uncharacteristic on April 9, 2009, when Iwata and head engineer Miyamoto appeared at the Foreign Correspondent's Club of Japan in central Tokyo ostensibly to discuss overseas strategy for the Wii and DS.

The results were, however, only marginally illuminating as they rehashed what to most industry watchers were well-known historical facts about the company. Other companies might jump at the opportunity to wax lyrical about their bright futures and bullish publicity initiatives. But Nintendo is reserved about making PR displays and fanning expectations beyond what they feel is necessary to sell their products. Perhaps this has a lot to do with a consistent corporate culture and constitution that has been maintained for so long. It isn't uncommon for Nintendo simply to announce in the most down-to-earth and staid terms nothing more than the title of a product and leave everyone standing in a shroud of mystery.

In keeping with this image, Kenji Toyoda, head of Nintendo's PR department, reflects the humility and self-deprecation the company is known for:

> We don't look at things in terms of winning or losing. If you look around you right now, some of the world's biggest-name companies are on the decline. It's just by luck that we find ourselves one length ahead at this point in time, and so we're not going to let that alter the way we do things.

"Doing your best, and leaving the rest to Heaven," is in the company name.

Toyoda is comfortable talking in a very matter-of-fact tone. On this day, he has come to report the company's third-quarter earnings. Splashed across the front page of one newspaper is the headline: "Nintendo to make downward revisions despite 300 billion yen profits, and industry lead."

"Our posture and perspective is always the same," Toyoda continues.

> We want to continue efforts to stay close to consumers and learn what gives them the most pleasure, similar to parents playing with their children, or teachers instructing their students on how to play with others, but do this through games. If the types of play we offer just so happen to move and excite a lot of people, and tell us that they had fun, we couldn't ask for anything more. It sounds simple, but let me assure you that we have plenty of cases of failures that reminds us it is not.

At this, Toyoda finally unwittingly grins. Perhaps the true measure of a company's strength lies in employees who can't speak of their company in unremarkable terms for too long before the thoughts and images swirling around in their head conjure up a smile.

Summary: Pride of Independence

It's easy to forget that Nintendo is an old company that dates back to humble beginnings in Kyoto in 1889. That's because the company didn't gain global fame until the 1980s a century later. It did so with the "Family Computer." The handheld console, DS Series, which debuted in 2004, had sold 100 million units by the end of

March 2009, while the Wii home gaming system has sold 50 million units, crowning Nintendo for the moment as undisputed leader of the computer gaming universe. Nintendo has for its part endured its share of failures as it strives to truly stir the hearts and minds of consumers. Through repeated failure and day-to-day accumulation of effort to produce a good product, the company's success thus may lie hidden in a stick-to-it work ethic and a go-it-alone style of management often attributed to Kyoto businesses.

"We have always tried to create new markets for our products. By developing a game console unlike any other before it, we have earned new customers in Japan and abroad," said senior executive Shigeru Miyamoto, who supervises Nintendo's software division, and was on hand on April 9, 2009 at the Foreign Correspondent's Club of Japan, together with company president, Satoru Iwata. They did make it a point to emphasize how their current products had succeeded in capturing new customers, particularly housewives and middle-age to elderly, who previously had never been familiar with or much interested in computer games. The Nintendo DS device flips open to reveal two liquid crystal display screens, one of which allows for direct writing with a stylus. The Wii home gaming system is controlled with a stick that you hold in one hand and shake or swing. It's all very easy and intuitive and invites anyone to play. Now the user base for computer game devices ranges from infants to senior citizens, and Iwata is the revolutionary whizkid much credited with changing the culture of "play."

In April 2009, Nintendo installed a front-facing and outward-facing camera in the DS along with audio player functionality and launched the DSi in the West. By further personalizing the DS to the user, Nintendo hopes its user base will spread from one unit per household to one unit per individual member.

"Maybe because we've remained in Kyoto all this time, we often use the term, 'Tokyo local.' If you're designing for popularity in Tokyo, you aren't making products that will travel globally. At any rate, it's important to make something that you don't see around you, since public reaction can change at the drop of a hat. If you do, you may have something that people will still praise several years down the road," said Miyamoto in an interview for the *Asahi* newspaper.

A lot of Kyoto companies have succeeded by employing a unique management style and unique technologies. A pride in independence is prevalent. There's no shortage of Kyoto entrepreneurs who believe that they can succeed if they do something different from how Tokyo people do it. It is a trait that is constituted by a strong sense of self and pride of craft built upon centuries of tradition, in what is Japan's traditional capital. Nintendo and Nintendo followers believe that ever since the computer game won support from a broad segment of the population, the computer game itself has earned a favorable reputation. It can be used for education, for rehabilitation, for communication. It has the potential for great social relevance. Nintendo's secret to success lies in an ability to distance itself from the maddening crowd, to learn from and endeavor through mistakes, and draw from within the knowledge and inspiration necessary to remain unique and valuable.

Principal Ideas of Satoru Iwata

- Always strive to create new markets.
- Seek to innovate and create things you don't readily see around you.
- Proceed without fear and go make the best gaming experience you can.

Nintendo Co., Ltd.

Established: November 20, 1947 (as Nintendo Co., Ltd.)

Satoru Iwata, President and CEO

Head office: 11-1, Kamitoba-hokodate-cho, Minami-ku, Kyoto City

http://www.nintendo.com/

Capital: 10,100 million yen (year ending March 2009)

Consolidated sales: 1,838,622 million yen

Consolidated operating profit: 555,263 million yen

Consolidated net profit: 279,089 million yen

Employees: 4,130

5

STANDING WITH CONSUMERS
ON DEREGULATED GROUND

Kaoru Seto
President
Yamato Holdings Co., Ltd.

Born November 1947 in Kanagawa Prefecture. Graduated from the
Faculty of Law at Chuo University and joined Yamato Transport Co. in
1970. Named executive officer in 1999, managing executive officer in
2004, then director of Yamato Transport and concurrent representative director of Yamato Holdings in 2005. Named president of Yamato
Holdings in June 2006.

One Man's Personality Saves a Company

Yamato Transport Co., Ltd. was founded in Tokyo in 1919 by
a young entrepreneur named Koshin Ogura who, starting with
only four trucks in the Tokyo metropolitan region, by 1960 had
built the biggest business to business courier service in the country.
But it was his son, Masao Ogura, a Tokyo University graduate who
in the 1970s would remake the company into the leading door-to-door
parcel delivery company it is today.

Masao Ogura was a man of rare perceptive ability, with hardy
nerves, who didn't fear failure and was considered the biggest people charmer in Japan. He avidly took to mentoring his staff and was
said to possess one of the most savvy business minds around.

Yet there was also an unorthodoxy to his thinking, as once expressed
in his view on hiring:

You can crunch numbers and analyze data all you want, but as long as it remains impossible to assess individual performance on a purely objective basis, you'll never really be able to tell just how good people are at their jobs. So it's somewhat meaningless when companies say that they "look for people who can get the job done." If, for argument's sake, you could single out such a person, how sure are you that he or she would be of benefit to your company?

Ogura always preferred to rely on a gut instinct style of hiring that emphasized long sit-down talks with people to get a feel for their personality. To him, it was no less reliable a method for assessing people than any other, and to its credit, those he put around him invariably proved to be hardworking self-starters who never complained about long hours, and comported themselves with what became known as the industry's highest levels of service and customer courtesy.

Perhaps this owed more to the personality of the man at the top of the organization than personnel screening techniques. For at every opportunity, Ogura could be seen gathering employees around him, particularly the younger ones, and engaging them in philosophical discussions.

"Don't place too much importance on whether you succeed in a venture," he might counsel them. "But have a passionate desire, instead, to learn how to succeed through one's endeavors."

Inside his company, Ogura worked to create a congenial and uncompetitive atmosphere. Unity took precedence over individual performance. This is because from the time of its inception, Yamato would have to mobilize its fighting spirit to engage in a long drawn-out battle against the status quo and government regulation. At the time, only the nationalized Japan Post provided door-to-door parcel and document delivery services.

Sensing Opportunity under Pressure

The company that Masao Ogura inherited from his father in 1971 was one whose fortunes were in decline. Yamato may have been a pioneer in building the nation's transport infrastructure, serving as courier to prestigious department store, Mitsukoshi, and top consumer appliance maker, Matsushita (now Panasonic). But by the 1970s, the company had been joined in the fray by many new rivals, which were now outpacing Yamato in the long-distance courier market. Matters only worsened with the Oil Crisis of 1973. By 1975, Yamato was teetering on the edge of oblivion.

In what amounted to a last-ditch effort to restore performance, Masao Ogura undertook a huge gambit to remake his company around a perceived need for door-to-door courier services. He imagined the convenience it would afford to individual households and homemakers, in particular. The idea itself wasn't groundbreaking. Most couriers had recognized its potential demand and considered it. But none could envision enough profit in the undertaking to justify the costs. Operations would be labor and capital intensive just like the business courier service, but only more so. It seemed a niche market at best, and because it would serve a somewhat amorphous and inconsistent customer base, it was potentially a logistical nightmare.

But Ogura was undeterred:

It is particularly in difficult times that opportunities present themselves. I figured if we could expand our distribution routes nationwide, and connect them with a network, we could build the business organically, by word of mouth, and sail past the breakeven point quickly.

Ogura believed this was the revival his company needed, as he imagined thousands of people all across the nation wishing for a way to get packages delivered to friends, family, and colleagues as fast as possible, faster than the state-run Japan Post and Japan National Railways.

"There are millions of homemakers out there," Ogura declared. "They want to send packages to their mothers back home; and mothers want to send gifts in return. If that exchange could be facilitated, made easier, more affordable, and convenient, I don't see any reason we couldn't get repeat customers."

Ogura was confident that success would spread like contagion once individual consumers across the nation experienced the elation and satisfaction of the service. But the start proved rocky. In the early going, Yamato might get only two calls a day. It would take some time before people learned that such a convenience even existed.

Fully prepared to incur some red ink, Ogura aggressively set to opening collection and dispatch offices all across the country, from metropolitan areas to the depopulated countryside, and then hunkered down for a protracted "winter campaign." To be sure, there were some horrendously performing outposts. But with each passing day, the ease and affordability of the service gradually began to make itself known, and largely by word of mouth.

Ogura delighted in hearing comments such as, "Yamato Transport is really useful. Even if all you've got is one package, they'll come pick it up with one phone call."

What Ogura had pioneered was the *takkyubin* business, basically, "home express delivery." As customers gravitated toward Yamato as a door-to-door express delivery specialist, *takkyubin* became a whole new business category of its own, and took root in the cultural vernacular.

Once the word was out, it became a matter of rapidly expanding service coverage to all regions. This became an imperative with the quick emergence of new rivals like Nippon Express, which quickly turned the new sector into a heated race for market share. Yamato upped the ante with more diversified and value-added services aimed at excavating more latent demand, such as "Ski Courier," "Golf Courier," "Cool Courier," and specific delivery time designation.

As Ogura had envisioned, growth in business volume rose alongside name recognition:

> Managers are paid to think. But sometimes you can rack your brains like mad, and still get no answers. There comes a point where you just have to throw in with your instincts and go for it. The good thing is that you're sure to learn something no matter what the results. Taking a trial-and-error approach doesn't always look good, but it will keep you on the path of progress.

The Courage to Change Course in Midstream

Masao Ogura assumed the company presidency from his father in what was certainly the biggest crisis in Yamato's history. The early 1970s saw Japan's age of rapid economic expansion draw to a close, hastened by US President Nixon's ending of the fixed exchange-rate system, his open-door policy with China, and two oil shocks. For Yamato, the ability to survive through these tumultuous times required drastic reforms in addition to the bold foray into a wholly new business. The workforce was reduced by 1,000 to 4,000 in total, and cost savings were sought wherever possible. Yet even these measures, as drastic as they were to those who had only known continuous growth, couldn't pull Yamato from the brink of bankruptcy.

For Ogura's survival plan to work, he felt he needed to increase service coverage, not pull back. The company served primarily the Kanto region: seven prefectures that contained or surrounded the Greater Tokyo Metropolitan area and represented an area of a little more than 131,000 square miles. Ogura's bold intentions naturally elicited surprise and stiff resistance among his officers. The company was teetering as it was, and it ran counter to common sense to seek further swelling of its deficits.

But Ogura stood firm, not because of some myopic delusion of grandeur or overconfidence in his own abilities, but because he saw real opportunity. Nearly all of the company's operations had been geared to dealing with large freight. It was a business that saw shrinking margins due to a glut of competitors and a slowing economy. Large freight was, of course, heavy and bulky. Ogura believed it was time to move away from a saturated market into a virtually untapped one in small freight. All that was needed was to shift the business model accordingly.

What kept people out of small parcel delivery was the conventional wisdom that, in contrast to large freight, one needed to be doing enormous volume in individual package transport to obtain the critical mass that would make it profitable. Just think of the multitude of delivery routes that would have to be established in the process. The fear was these factors would certainly lead to inefficient, unreliable and inconsistent service, which would prove too costly, and would turn off customers.

But Ogura balanced these concerns against the potential upside. "On the other hand, homemakers wouldn't constantly be asking for rate discounts like commercial clients do. It would be a cash-based operation. The idea that cash could be earned on the spot made it all exceedingly attractive. Plus our business as it was would only get worse, and I much preferred to try something new than to sit around waiting for the ball to drop."

Thus came a singular turning point in the company's history, if not for the distribution sector in general. Yamato Transport retooled itself for a new business, and went from a near-bankrupt company to an industry leader boasting a trillion yen in sales.

Before we came along, if people wanted to mail a package, they had to carry it to their local post office. But even then, they were met with a maximum weight limit of six kilograms (15 pounds) per item. If, for example, parents who lived in the countryside wanted to send a care package to a son or daughter living and working in Tokyo, there was no indication nor guarantee as to what day and at what time that package would arrive. There was clearly room for improvement here. I thought senders and recipients deserved a little more. Surely, we could give them greater convenience, reliability and peace of mind than they were used to getting, at a great price.

Fighting the Good Fight

Masao Ogura's well-intentioned and earnest response to a latent demand was indeed eagerly welcomed by the ordinary citizens to whom it was directed. With tremendous speed, Yamato *takkyubin* trucks and delivery people grew into established icons in communities all across the nation, as they served a growing, ubiquitous need. And the company's earnings bent sharply upward as a result.

While Yamato was being hailed as a hero among the citizenry, it was viewed banefully in government circles. Ogura had chosen to do battle with some powerful foes, namely, the (then) Ministry of Posts and Communications and the national rail company. The government simply couldn't keep pace with the rate of innovation that Yamato was deploying for the convenience of the consumer. Moreover, all of the new services Ogura and company were releasing into the market were hitting their mark, building customer trust. With every new move, Ogura would find himself met by ministry officials demanding his compliance to some arcane regulation, or checking his progress with red tape. But Ogura, driven by his convictions of what was right, good and necessary, never yielded to the pressure.

As would be expected, Yamato's successful model for express door-to-door parcel delivery was followed by an onslaught of new combatants. Ogura welcomed this as good for competition and for solidifying the viability of the industry. It would lead to better service and higher quality standards at the cost of those who failed to innovate, such as the state-run Japanese National Railways, which saw its door-to-door service disappear within 10 years of Yamato's emergence in the sector. Japan Post couldn't idly watch a major earnings component slip from its grasp, and eventually launched their own dedicated domestic parcel service called "Yu-pack."

Gone now were the days when the government enjoyed a virtual monopoly on parcel delivery in the nation. The rise of Yamato *takkyubin* and other operators had opened consumer eyes to what parcel delivery service could be.

But Yamato's battle with Japan Post would continue. In 2004, a major convenience store chain, Lawson, began handling Japan Post parcels, adding close to 8,000 more outlets for the service to the 20,000 post offices the government body already operated nationwide. Yamato cried foul, seeking an injunction to prevent the tieup as a violation of the Antimonopoly Law, since Japan Post could offer lower prices because of preferential tax treatment and other benefits it enjoyed.

Yamato's determination not to yield on this matter, either, helped fuel a growing debate in parliament over whether Japan's postal service should ultimately be privatized to encourage competition. Newspapers and editorials favoring the move had splashed headlines labeling the government-run body as an unfair monopoly. Lawson eventually pulled out of the contract.

The controversial privatization of Japan Post to the Japan Post Service Company in 2007 was welcomed by many but not Yamato, which saw its long, hard-fought battle with government evolve into an even more daunting challenge: the overnight emergence of a powerful rival with a replete ready-to-go infrastructure already in place. With 24,600 large and small post offices around the country, it more than doubled the number of retail outlets for the nation's largest convenience store, 7-Eleven, making the Japan Post Service Company the country's largest chain business.

"We tried everything we could to ensure a level playing field in lieu of the post privatization," recalls current Yamato president, Kaoru Seto. "But we were up against a powerful foe. Still, we were encouraged and fortified by a fighting spirit that rose through the ranks of our company. There were people saying that our 100-year history had made lions of us. We weren't going to be defeated, and the whole company seemed to rise in unity to fight the good fight, as it always has."

Building a Symbiotic Environment

Masao Ogura passed away at the age of 80 in June 2005. A year later, the baton was passed to Kaoru Seto, a man who shares Ogura's keen sense of perspective and trailblazing instinct to craft new strategies that can create new growth and keep Yamato the industry leader. One of his first efforts has been a strategy dubbed "Operation Centipede," aimed at actively bolstering ties with group and client companies to tap new demand for goods and services that led to more parcel deliveries.

Since the global economic downturn in late 2008, Yamato has seen demand for express parcel delivery drop for the first time since the business began in 1976, prompting many analysts to think that the industry has reached a plateau. But just as the arrival to Japan of online bookseller, Amazon.com, boosted demand for home delivery of books and other products, Yamato is taking on an active role in using the strengths of group companies, such as its digital electronics repair center and mail order logistic services, not only to increase Yamato deliveries, but also to shorten delivery times. Essentially, Yamato Holdings receives commissions by companies to handle everything from warehousing of goods purchased online or by TV shopping to e-money settlements through its 6,000 direct delivery drivers. Through such efforts, Yamato hopes to increase customer convenience and drastically reduce delivery times to as little as four hours between some online orders and delivery.

> I tell my people to view the diversification of consumer demand (amid declines in overall consumption) as a great growth opportunity. We need to be right on top of that demand and meet it with improved delivery speed and quality.

One solution is to narrow the geographical territory covered by each driver by locating collection and dispatch posts close enough together to ensure that deliveries are never more than 10–15 minutes away. This way, a system could be built to guarantee most daily deliveries be made by no later than noon. But if a delivery is not received, a second delivery attempt is never more than 15 minutes away.

Seto continues:

> Narrowing the territory per driver will add to the number of drivers we need. But you can counterbalance that with the added convenience to customers in quick and immediate deliveries, and also decrease what we call "idle running time," when vehicles must travel long distances only to return without having made their delivery. Having one driver cover a larger area might seem more cost effective, but it is not. So we are constantly examining new ways to generate efficiencies that will benefit everyone.

If the express parcel delivery market that Yamato pioneered in 1976 has finally leveled off after years of double-digit growth, the next age of growth will have to come through innovations in service content such as greater specialization, more diverse pricing, or the exploitation of new demand.

Like company founder Koshin Ogura, and his son, Masao, it will be up to Kaoru Seto and subsequent leaders like him to extend Yamato Transport Company's tradition of fearlessness through adversity and its indomitable spirit deep into the twenty-first century.

Summary: Still a Leader, Still an Innovator

When the late Masao Ogura, second president of the Tokyo-based Yamato Transport Company (now Yamato Holdings), transformed his company into a door-to-door express parcel delivery service targeting mainly individuals and small businesses, he was giving birth to a new industry that would become as ubiquitous as the postal service.

Current company president Kaoru Seto, who joined Yamato in 1970, was the youngest member to take part in the early development of the *takkyubin* business. He would then lead the introduction of a host of new services, such as "Cool Takkyubin," that earned commercial success and put Yamato atop its industry where it remains today.

Yamato owes its success in *takkyubin* to constant product development, a process that was so formative in Seto's early career that it stands at the heart of his current "Operation Centipede" to meet new demand by actively extending its "arms and legs" in various directions ultimately to boost parcel deliveries. In 2008, Seto articulated the Yamato Group image succinctly and accurately as: "Still a Leader, Still an Innovator."

Seto was a mere 27 years old when he was tapped by President Masao Ogura to join the project team in the development of the country's first door-to-door express parcel service. Yamato Transport at the time was suffering. The oil crises of 1973 and 1974 had triggered an economic malaise throughout Japan, leading to shortages of petroleum-based daily goods and long lines at supermarkets. As a trucking company that relied heavily on large freight transport, Yamato watched its revenues plummet. Ogura couldn't see the company surviving much longer in a business that was growing more unprofitable by the day.

"If we can't expect things to improve no matter how much we try, then it's time to try something else."

Ogura coalesced a team around a plan to build a collection and distribution network for small parcel deliveries to individual households and small businesses, for which per-unit freight charges would be low, but revenue stability could be expected. The concept Ogura drafted consisted of five major points:

- Target an indefinite but potentially large number of individual "cargo owners" (customers) and their cargo.
- Adopt a customer/user perspective in all matters.
- Provide and maintain consistent, superior service.
- Ensure the system is durable and progressive in nature.
- Work to boost efficiency at all times.

The door-to-door express parcel delivery idea was initially rebuffed by many as a logistical nightmare that would consume far too much time and labor in fulfilling small delivery orders across scattered and far-flung destinations. Demand for the service did certainly exist, but it was serviced only by state-run postal service and national rail companies. The level of service left much to be desired. Small packages to and from individuals took several days for delivery, and users were saddled with many painstaking rules in the packaging process. In offering a privately run, door-to-door delivery service, therefore, Yamato found several natural opportunities for gaining an advantage. For starters, collection stations and business offices would be established in residential districts. A large fleet of trucks would be deployed to circulate through each territory collecting and delivering packages among private households and local businesses. Simple and convenient packaging on the part of the customer would suffice. Next-day deliveries would be the norm and a fixed-rate scale by region would be applied.

When the new business was launched, the entire fortunes of the company rested on its success. Yet on the first day, Yamato received only 11 calls. After the first month, they'd made less than 9,000 deliveries—a discouragingly slow start. But those who did try the new service, drawn by its "next-day delivery" claims, found it a refreshing switch to the alternative. Word spread of a convenient new way to send packages, and as the *takkyubin* gradually began to attain critical customer mass, Yamato went ahead and opened more collection offices, increased delivery rounds, and raised pickup and delivery speeds, for there was always plenty of room for improvement.

Yamato bought television commercial time to run ads telling people about a service in which one simple phone call would bring a delivery man to your home to pick up your packages. Sustained product development and persistence began to pay off as consumers grew increasingly aware of the service, and the volume of cargo handled began to grow exponentially.

"We had no idea what the reaction would be at first," recalls Seto, who was part of the development team. As he made his way to the various offices, and transferred his own business base to Yokohama, the rapid growth in customers amazed him.

"Who'd have thought there was such a need for this?" he remembers musing. As demand grew, further needs came into view, and Seto would spend the bulk of his rising career thinking of ways to improve the service. When he was transferred to Fukuoka on Japan's southern island of Kyushu, he encountered reams of customers eager to send packages of local delicacies and products, such as spicy cod roe and handcrafted dolls to friends, families, and colleagues around the country.

Upon his return to Tokyo, Seto developed a refrigerated items delivery service, chilled or frozen, called "Cool Takkyubin." When later he was promoted to labor division chief, Seto developed a work shift planning system based on a logistical formula that would ensure that each business office had just the right number of staff on hand at any given time, and employing part-time workers to serve as sorters at each consolidation point while constantly streamlining to reduce work load per sorter and truck driver. All was designed to ensure quicker and better service.

As a student, Kaoru Seto had worked a variety of part-time jobs, including temp labor, carpenter, newspaper office boy, and even department store parcel delivery staff member. From these experiences, he says he learned the value of individual resourcefulness and ingenuity in the field. Even with good pay, very few will choose to stick with monotonous jobs where one is merely a cog in the machine. Seto believed that jobs demanding a little creativity: a chance to dream up solutions to problems experienced in the field, and receiving first-hand the favorable response of customers to the results of those creative efforts is what made work enjoyable and rewarding. To this day, Seto places a premium on "*genba*-ism" (dedication to the field or shop floor) and use of the knowledge gained there as creative grist for new products and services that respond to new demand or improved efficiencies. "*Genba*-ism" is a common philosophical thread running through the stories of most successful Japanese businesses, and Seto's "Operation Centipede" provides a prime practical example.

Yamato's response to the global economic recession that began in 2008 is to leverage its rich know-how in the parcel delivery business to grow into a comprehensive business solutions company that fuses functions in logistics technology, IT, and financial technology, offering merchandisers and customers as quick as four-hour delivery turnaround on online orders, and giving businesses access to warehousing systems that operate 24 hours a day, 365 days a year.

At the end of fiscal year 2007 (ending March 2008), door-to-door parcel delivery still accounted for one trillion of Yamato's 1.225 trillion yen in consolidated earnings, But Kaoru Seto and Yamato will be looking to change that ratio significantly in the coming years.

Principal Ideas of Kaoru Seto

- Target that which may be indefinite but harbors immense potential.
- Be passionate about achieving success through your own endeavor.
- Place a premium on "*genba*-ism" (dedication to the field or shop floor).

Yamato Holdings Co., Ltd.

Established: April 9, 1929
Kaoru Seto, President
Head office: 2-16-10, Ginza, Chuo-ku, Tokyo
http://www.kuronekoyamato.co.jp/english/
Capital: 120,728 million yen (year ending March 2009)
Consolidated sales: 1,251,921 million yen
Consolidated operating profit: 55,720 million yen
Consolidated net profit: 25,523 million yen
Employees: 170,664

6

FROM JAPAN TO THE WORLD'S DINNER TABLES

Yuzaburo Mogi
Chairman and CEO
Kikkoman Corp.

Born 1935, Yuzaburo Mogi received a Bachelor of Arts from Keio University in 1958 and an MBA from Columbia University in 1961. In 1958, began professional career with Kikkoman Corporation, which was founded by his ancestors in the seventeenth century. Appointed president and CEO in 1995 and has been chairman and CEO since 2004. Served as vice chairman of Keizai Doyukai (Japan Association of Corporate Executives). Currently serves as the co-chairman of the National Congress for the 21st Century Japan, honorary ambassador of the State of Wisconsin, US, Japanese chairman of the German–Japanese Forum, chairman of the Japan–Midwest US Association, trustee emeritus of Columbia University, and trustee of Keio University. For his achievements, Yuzaburo Mogi was awarded the Medal of Honor with Blue Ribbon of Japan in 1999 and distinguished with the Order of Orange Nassau from the Kingdom of the Netherlands in 2003.

An All-Purpose Seasoning

During the hundred years between the mid-seventeenth century to the mid-eighteenth century, soy sauce production led by the Mogi and Takanashi families prospered in the city of Noda in Chiba Prefecture. With many geographic advantages, Noda was blessed with two major waterways: the Tone and Edo rivers, which facilitated the development of boat transport and the transportation of ingredients, while manufactured products could be delivered to nearby Edo for mass consumption.

In 1917, the Mogi family, the Takanashi family and the Horikiri family merged their businesses to form Noda Shoyu Co. Each had its own individual soy sauce brands, but decided to use the most well-known brand name among them at the time, Kikkoman.

For the origins of soy sauce itself, one has to go back to about the sixth century when a type of soy sauce was brought over to Japan from China. In contrast to Chinese-made soy sauce, made only from soybeans, the Japanese variety contained wheat, which gave it a distinctively deep flavor and fragrance. In the many centuries that followed, a uniquely Japanese soy sauce culture developed.

Japan didn't start exporting soy sauce abroad until the period between 1647 and 1668 when it was loaded onto Dutch ships leaving ports in Nagasaki for India. There are documents attributing the beginning of soy sauce exports to the Dutch East India Company. Japan at the time was in the midst of a government-enforced, 200-year closed-door policy (*sakoku*), in which the only foreign trade allowed was with the Dutch, and only through the ports in Nagasaki.

Documentation from that time indicates that even trade with the Dutch was miniscule, so the opportunities for carrying soy sauce out of the country were exceedingly limited. The soy sauce that did make it all the way to northern Europe as a Japanese import was given the moniker "liquid spice." But the East India Company gave the Dutch ample opportunities to come in contact with a wide variety of spices and condiments, and among them, soy sauce in particular had a strong reception.

The flow of soy sauce would continue unabated as Japanese began to emigrate abroad in the years after, first to Hawaii, then to San Francisco, and all along the west coast of the US. After Japan's defeat in the Pacific War in 1945, American expatriates and GIs of the allied occupation grew attached to the flavor, and would pack it with them on their return home.

Americans were easily won over by the sauce's ability to bring out the natural flavors of meat. When Kikkoman rented out a floor of a Japanese department store in San Francisco and opened a make-shift "sukiyaki restaurant," long lines formed, prompting *The San Francisco Chronicle* to write about it under a headline describing Kikkoman Soy Sauce as an "All-Purpose Seasoning!"

Seeing this, a Kikkoman representative was so impressed by the response and the writeup that he decided to make the headline the product slogan. Since that time, "all-purpose seasoning" graces every bottle of Kikkoman soy sauce both at home and abroad.

Yuzaburo Mogi's Power of Persuasion

The man most responsible for Kikkoman's global pervasiveness is Yuzaburo Mogi, a descendant of one of the families of the eight founders. As a young man, Yuzaburo displayed a passionate interest in business, reading every book on management he could get his hands on. As a college student, he was particularly impressed by the writings of Austria-born business guru, Peter F. Drucker and his emphasis on the individual consumer.

Upon graduating from Keio University in Tokyo, Mogi joined the family-run Noda Shoyu Company (now Kikkoman Corporation). Yearning to learn business from where it was practiced and taught best, Mogi set off to the US to attend Columbia University's School of Business. He graduated in 1961 and became the first Japanese to receive an MBA from the school.

From early on, Mogi had begun to formulate his own philosophy toward business:

> When working toward an objective, it is absolutely imperative that you be able to convince people, first inside your company, then outside your company of the value of what you're trying to accomplish. This is no mean feat. Convincing people who already have established patterns of thinking is difficult. Therefore, I think the power of persuasion hinges greatly on presentation. If you hope to win people over, you need to convey information and ideas in such a way that they can't help but start nodding in understanding. Moreover, you must have a very clear idea of what it is you want to do yourself, what you need to do, and have a firm grasp of the whole picture.

Mogi sought to use the power of presentation to open the American consumer's eyes to his product. This took the form of carrying around a gas burner to supermarkets, cutting small slices of beef with soy sauce and serving them to shoppers. Mogi undertook many demonstrations like this involving direct communications with shoppers to educate them on how to cook meals with "soy sauce," basically saying in point-blank fashion, "This is the what I'm offering. What do you think?" Nearly everybody who tasted his samples,

Mogi says, walked away persuaded, and he quickly sold all the stock he had brought.

Success in marketing a uniquely Japanese seasoning to the world drew considerable attention to the outspoken Mogi himself, with people seeking him out for his business insights:

> I often got asked to share my secrets, based on Kikkoman's experience, on how to succeed as a global company. I had to tell them quite frankly and bluntly that we had no special know-how or step-by-step recipe for conducting a successful global strategy. We simply took things one step at a time in what amounted to a recurring process of trial and error; the results of which might or might not open new doors. But one thing I will say is that when we saw a good opportunity, we never failed to seize it. As long as you have a clear objective, you'll be able to see plenty of opportunities to achieve it.

Most Japanese companies since 2000, and particularly since the worldwide recession in 2008, have come to view globalization of operations as a new imperative for their survival. But it is not a course that businesses can readily set for themselves. A firm needs to be able to foster the kinds of people who can perform on a global stage. Going abroad to compete with foreign players and appeal to foreign customers requires patience and an open mind:

> Before Kikkoman's success in the US, we actually began our overseas expansion by targeting people of Japanese descent living in Hawaii. We didn't exactly consider that as having an overseas presence. It wasn't even an export business yet. It was something much more intimate and limited in scale: a marketing expedition. As time went on, our products began to get noticed by Americans coming to Japan for visit or work. What we saw was encouraging in terms of poten-tial demand for our products. The US in the mid-1950s was this awe-inspiring, enormous economic power. We could see signs that in such a colossal market, we might find a warm welcome.

Kikkoman's establishment of a sales company in San Francisco would prove the critical launching pad for expanding bases of operations across the country.

The Importance of Exchange and Union

Times of soaring oil prices wreak havoc on the global economy, but the effects are particularly devastating and pervasive in natural resource deficient Japan. In the period leading up to the global financial meltdown in 2008, expensive crude oil drove up food prices in Japan, and having always been deeply concerned with consumer needs, the crisis heightened Mogi's consumer consciousness all the more:

> For over a decade now, Japan had been caught up in a deflationary·spiral. Now suddenly we're seeing unavoidable rises in the price of goods and services. This is quite common in the US to the extent that consumers don't make too much of it. But in Japan, it's treated as front-page news. Each country has its own way of thinking about prices. So rather than having these price changes foisted on people unilaterally, there is a great need for us to confront the situation together with all stakeholders, starting with consumers to retailers, so there is sufficient understanding.

Simply passing rising costs onto the consumer is the quickest way to lose customers, Mogi believes. So there must be a dialogue between companies and customers about the necessity of raising prices:

> Companies cannot expect to sell their products and services over the long term by simply asking consumers to buy them. There must be an exchange taking place. Kikkoman soy sauce is produced in seven locations across the globe, and is distributed to more than 100 countries. With every bottle of soy sauce that we sell, we are also winning acceptance of a part of Japanese daily life. Every time a family member reaches for the soy sauce at the dinner table, there is a cultural exchange. If we continue to nourish that exchange further, a union of cultural values can take place. So it always reminds us of the great importance of increasing contacts with people and promoting cultural exchange.

Don't Fall into Conventional Molds

The harsh reality among many Japanese companies is that domestic demand is steadily shrinking. But that doesn't mean one has to scale back. There are always ways to grow. In April 2008, Kikkoman welcomed in a new president, Mitsuo Someya, who quickly clarified his company's strategy going forward:

> Consumers already know and expect Kikkoman products to be good. In other words, it's not enough for them to taste good. We need to further elevate their value. It is important that we offer products that legions of consumers acknowledge as delicious plus something else.
>
> If I were to present a specific example of our company's actual ongoing efforts in this area, one is that we are making products that address the increased health consciousness of consumers, particularly since the government mandated more nationally standardized health checkups.
>
> Vegetable juice from our Del Monte brand and the soy milk products of the FoodChemifa Company are good examples. We think demand for these products will grow even faster in the future, and we want to help accelerate that.

As a company that succeeded overseas early, Kikkoman is not averse to the idea of strategic merger and acquisition (M&A) activities. But the operative word is "caution:"

> Yes, we are of course always on the lookout for strong synergies between companies. But the risk for our company in bringing in an unrelated business would be too great. We're not thinking any further other than an M&A that would help our core business and specialty in brewing and fermentation. By keeping our focus, we can expand our existing capabilities and opportunities, and look to fortify our brand strength from its core.

Kikkoman celebrated its fiftieth year in the US in 2007. The company continues to enjoy strong earnings and growth, selling not only soy sauce and other condiments, but also dietary supplements and enzymes produced at its biotech division. One region in which Kikkoman harbors high expectations is Europe, where sales for Kikkoman products have been growing at double-digit rates. In the company's Global Vision 2020, Someya spelled out his desire to expand market reach to central and eastern Europe, including Russia:

> Our strategy for Europe is still in the developmental stages. We're hoping that soy sauce will play an increasingly greater

role in the European market and replace other traditional seasonings. To do that, we need to raise its profile. One way we're trying to do that is to concentrate on products that use or are related to soy sauce, such as teriyaki sauce, and look to expand the market that way.

Kikkoman has focused on both global reach and product diversification at home and abroad. The company is famous for being one of the first Japanese food companies to take its products overseas, long before people talked regularly of globalization. Nearly half of Kikkoman's earnings come from overseas, with consumption actually higher abroad than it is in Japan. But as domestic competitors make their way abroad, and major food companies increase in size, Kikkoman has put diversification at the top of its priorities in its global and local strategies. Kikkoman has long known it could not rely only on soy sauce sales. For that reason, it formed the Manns Wine Company as far back as 1964 and began producing its own wine. By developing many strong food products under the Del Monte label, Kikkoman has made Del Monte as much of a household name in Japan as Kikkoman:

> It's easy to use the word "diversification," but there are many ways to think about it. Of course you should go with something that holds out the most benefits such as: Can we expect synergies with our core business? Or will there be cross-interference? Can we take advantage of our existing know-how? We decided quite early on not to be just a soy sauce company, and yet we still want to focus on our expertise in seasonings and food products. We've found that as we pursue this, we are reminded of how much soy sauce has become a fixture on dinner tables. Kikkoman soy sauce is used by millions of people in more than 100 countries. It has become the world's seasoning.

Summary: Forget Nationality, Try Universality

With a history that dates back to 1661, Kikkoman is one of Japan's oldest surviving companies. It began as an eight-family-operated business making soy sauce which quickly became an indispensable item in the Japanese diet along with rice, vegetables, and fish. But

Kikkoman's ability to increase sales and revenues continually over its long history owes less to selling a standard household product to Japanese consumers than to an aggressive overseas marketing strategy, beginning with the biggest market of them all: the US. Early on, Kikkoman sought to earn the understanding and devotion of consumers around the world as a great all-purpose seasoning for meat, poultry, and fish dishes, aggressively going ahead to build a soy sauce brewery in the US in 1972.

"I remember the Tokyo bureau chief of the *Washington Post* coming to visit me and telling me that until arriving in Japan, he had no idea that Kikkoman was a Japanese company. Those were exactly the kinds of words I wanted to hear," muses Kikkoman CEO Yuzaburo Mogi.

While earning an MBA from Columbia University, the first by a Japanese national, Yuzaburo Mogi spent his free time going to various supermarkets to see whether they carried Kikkoman soy sauce, how the products were being displayed, and observing who bought the products and with what other groceries.

The company carried out a variety of promotional campaigns, including cooking small slices of beef in supermarkets, dipping them in soy sauce, and passing them out on toothpicks to shoppers, or introducing quick and easy recipes using soy sauce in television commercials during time slots where homemakers would most likely be watching. Soy sauce gradually found its way into the American market and consciousness. Upon his return to Japan, Mogi spearheaded the initiative to locally produce Kikkoman products in the US, and followed that with production plants in Europe and China. Having been educated in the US, Mogi became an outspoken proponent of rational Western business practices, such as deregulation, risk taking and incentive-based pay for executives. One thing he was particularly proud of was that as Kikkoman laid down operational roots in the US and elsewhere, consumers forgot that it was a Japanese company.

Atop a flagpole outside the front entrance of the Kikkoman soy sauce plant in Walworth, Wisconsin, a large American flag flutters in the wind. Kikkoman was one of the earliest Japanese companies to break from creating enclaves of Japanese employees and citizens within larger foreign communities. It instead wanted to sink roots abroad and partner with local citizens as neighbors.

At one point, when the decision was made to expand operations abroad in largely conservative agriculture-based communities, the company did encounter some opposition in the form of misconceived fears that soybeans were unkind to the soil. Mogi made public rounds through those communities, shaking hands, and visiting homes and organizations as he earnestly and honestly discussed his intentions and dispelled such rumors, eventually earning him respect and understanding from even the most intractable and unapproachable rural elements. From this experience, Mogi was able to solidify his belief that "nothing is born without putting yourself on the line and taking a little risk."

Principal Ideas of Yuzaburo Mogi

- If you have clear objectives, you'll see plenty of opportunity.
- Grow as locally as possible.
- Nothing great comes without putting yourself out there and taking a little risk.

Kikkoman Corp.

Established: December 1917
Yuzaburo Mogi, Chairman and CEO
Mitsuo Someya, President and COO
Head office: 250, Noda, Noda City, Chiba
http://www.kikkoman.com/
Capital: 11,600 million yen (year ending March 2009)
Consolidated sales: 412,649 million yen
Consolidated operating profit: 20,368 million yen
Consolidated net profit: 2,746 million yen
Employees: 5,226

7

MATCHING BRICK-AND-MORTAR INNOVATION WITH THE IT REVOLUTION

Tadashi Yanai
Founder, President and CEO
Fast Retailing Co., Ltd.

Born February 1949 in Yamaguchi Prefecture, Japan, and a graduate of the School of Political Science and Economics at Waseda University, Tadashi Yanai spent nine months after college in the employment of supermarket super store chain JUSCO (now AEON Retail Co., Ltd.) before going to work for his father's men's apparel company, Men's Shop Ogori Shoji. When he took over management of the company in 1984, Yanai changed its name to Unique Clothing Warehouse (Uniqlo, for short) and launched its flagship store in Hiroshima city. The name was changed again in 1991 to Fast Retailing, and was listed on the Tokyo Stock Exchange's First Section (for large companies) in 1999. In 2009, Yanai topped the Forbes list of Japan's 40 Richest Businesspeople with an estimated net worth of $6.1 billion. He represents the changing face of Japanese management.

A Youth Who Failed to See the Profit in Business

Tadashi Yanai's professional career had its humble beginnings at a men's retail and wholesale suit company in a quiet town near the southern tip of Japan's Honshu island. The business was his father's, and Yanai had grown up watching his dad run it. Like most children, Yanai didn't take a particular interest in his father's work, and even after college graduation never pictured himself taking over the family business.

Although Yanai was not the eldest of three children, he was the eldest son, which traditionally meant that he inherited the right and "duty" of primogeniture. But those who knew young Tadashi at the time saw in him a person who didn't seem at all burdened by such outdated norms and pressures, owing to his own disposition and the lack of such pressure from his parents.

Yet Yanai still found reason to distance himself from his father's business, not to be free from the pull of home, but because he never quite agreed with his father's management philosophy. It seemed to be too focused on money.

"A business that isn't about money is like a person without a head," his father had said to him. Yanai had found that bit of wisdom disturbing. For he had grown up feeling the effects that his father's business had on his daily life, which gave him very visceral, if not yet well-formed ideas, about business.

"I felt an aversion to the way my father ran his company," recalls Yanai. "Chalk some of that up to being young and rebellious. But it certainly wasn't the career I envisioned for myself. In fact, the world had yet to excite me at all."

Yanai cites the lack of external stimulation in his hometown as one factor for his apathy. Yamaguchi is among the bottom half of Japan's prefectures in population density:

> There just wasn't much to do, and very little to inspire big dreams. I would get together with friends and kill time by playing mahjong. Sometimes, we'd play for three days straight without batting an eye. I don't look back on those times as having been a waste. I was youthful and carefree. But I also possessed no drive. I harbored no particular hopes or great vision of the future, but instead felt content with the idea that I could go through life simply getting by without too much thought or effort, and that would be perfectly fine.

This seems in stark contrast to Tadashi Yanai today, who is famous for being something of a hard driver at work and has little patience for anyone who doesn't demonstrate sincerity or passion about his or her work. Yanai is known to never mince words. It is not uncommon to see the president in the face of an employee, chewing him out for indolence or lack of motivation. To many who know him now, Yanai's aimlessness as a youth comes as a surprise.

"I figured something would come along without too much effort," Yanai remembers. "But it never did. The only skills I had developed by the time I left school were playing mahjong and *pachinko* [a casino-style pinball game]. I wasn't particularly fond of gambling. There just simply was little else to do."

Yanai returned home to Yamaguchi Prefecture after college, believing that if he was going to waste time, it would be cheaper to do so in the countryside rather than in Tokyo. He did manage to land a job at a department store and supermarket chain called JUSCO (now AEON Group), but quit within a year. Rather than trying to force himself into a particular direction, Yanai decided on a wait-and-see approach to life. That is when he found himself back at his father's store, as an employee.

Needless to say, this proved to be the critical turning point that he was seeking, and it happened right at home. For the first time, Yanai began thinking in specifics about what it was his father did for a living, and subsequently, harboring doubts:

Once I started helping out at my father's store, I found myself drawing comparisons with my previous job at JUSCO. Though I hadn't worked there long, I still underwent a thorough and rigorous training program, which thankfully gave me enough insight and varied perspective to see that my dad ran things quite differently from JUSCO, and quite inefficiently, too. It was then that I realized my father would never make any money. There was a lot of waste in his business methods, which translated directly into losses. It was eye opening for sure. But the biggest surprise was yet to come. When I finally confronted my father to inform him of all the things I thought he was doing wrong with the business, he sat quietly and listened. As soon as I finished speaking my mind, he stood up and handed me the registered seal to his company and said, "The shop is yours."

From that moment, it was as though a fire had been lit inside Yanai, and he proceeded to throw himself wholly into learning all he could about the clothing business and business in general. He devoured books by Matsushita Electric Industrial (Panasonic

Corporation) founder Konosuke Matsushita, and Honda Motor Company founder Soichiro Honda, not caring that these men hailed from different industries. Yanai needed to learn the management philosophies of the great companies: the ones that were leaving their mark on the world.

"I resolved to set a target for each day, and to keep score of everything," recalls Yanai. "I saw how there were often recurring patterns of good and bad times, and the more I began to study and understand the results, the more interesting the idea of running a business became."

Yanai rapidly began to acquire his own feel for how he might run things, which included a healthy inquisitiveness. The biggest question that nagged him was whether it was meaningful to stay focused on men's clothing, particularly suits. In secret, he had been nursing an idea to sell casual clothes, and he felt that the chances of success in that realm would be far greater, the opportunities much more numerous:

> Switching to casual clothing would expand our customer base. Casual clothes are worn by everybody. While we would never regard them as household consumables like groceries, there is much greater potential for moving products every day.

The shift in product required a catchy new name to describe it, and Yanai went with Unique Clothing Warehouse (Uniqlo). He now wielded a much broader palate to work with in dreaming up new business strategies, and the ideas began to flow with such frequency and intensity that his days of passive torpidity seemed now a world away.

From Product Handler to Innovator

"Cheaper means inferior" has been the prevailing belief among quality-sensitive Japanese consumers. "If a product is cheap in price," notes Yanai, "there's got to be a catch. Because price and quality are directly correlated."

That is what customers immediately communicated to Yanai as soon as he began selling casual clothes. On the other hand, customers seek value, too. If they know that they can buy a high-quality product for even one yen less than the market price, they will. "Providing that value poses a difficult challenge, but it's one well worth pursuing."

By the time Yanai's Uniqlo entered the market, there was already a spate of large retailers charging ahead with small-margin, high-volume retail business models. The bursting of the asset bubble in Japan in the early 1990s had sent the economy reeling into a deep and protracted recession. It weakened consumer confidence and purchasing power, forcing many to shirk luxury brands for the best values they could find. Mass-market department store operators such as Daiei and Ito-Yokado sought to capitalize quickly on this trend by opening new stores and expanding floor space. Major foreign franchises such as Gap entered the once prohibitive Japanese market with a vengeance.

But that didn't deter Yanai. Instead, he adopted a strategy of buying up large supplies of strong-selling products that apparel makers tended to overproduce. He also started purchasing directly from manufacturers, bypassing a lot of intermediaries. This not only saved time and money, but also enabled Yanai to keep pace with trends in real time, and focus on only fast-moving inventory.

With an ample amount of the right products at the right time, all that was needed was a sustained marketing effort that would enable Yanai to build a strong base of consumer support. Uniqlo needed to carve out a niche for itself; a concept with which it could be easily and uniquely identified. That concept materialized in a method of stocking only popular fashion items in great abundance and variety; and then offering them to consumers at anywhere from 10 to 20 percent lower than the market average.

The success achieved with this model gave Yanai the traction he needed to launch a full-scale assault on the mass-market fashion industry. New Uniqlo shops began opening all over Japan, and while Yanai worked to overcome growing pains such as streamlining existing distribution, he also saw a need to build and diversify his product portfolio to prevent the company from becoming a flash-in-the-pan, one-trick pony.

That was when he glanced across the Sea of Japan at the sheer human power and cost savings of China. Joining forces with Chinese factories gave Uniqlo the opportunity it needed to begin making its own clothing: a necessary next step in the growth of the company.

When you're selling other people's products, the only real wiggle room you have with customers is in pricing. How much cheaper can you afford to sell the same products that your competitors are selling? You can only expect to sustain the upper hand for so long before those cheaper prices become standard in the mind of the consumer, or for as long as you can prevent price gouging from sinking to levels where you fail to meet consumer expectations of value. So we knew that if we could start making and selling our own in-house-developed products, that would add another value proposition to the mix besides price.

Sure enough, once prices began to level off, Yanai turned his attention to differentiation. Could Uniqlo truly distinguish itself and generate excitement for its products for reasons other than price? Yes, there would be a heavy emphasis on good product design. And utility. These clothes were expected to live up to heavy use by consumers. So Yanai and his team went in search of new ideas.

Uniqlo had extended its reach throughout the country. But it had yet to arrive in the biggest market of all: Tokyo. In the fall of 2001, six years after opening the first Uniqlo roadside store, Yanai officially changed his company name from Ogori Shoji to Fast Retailing Co., Ltd. to serve as a holding company, of which Uniqlo would be its main subsidiary. As Fast Retailing, particularly the Uniqlo clothing brand, began to generate more attention and press coverage, its debut in the nation's capital became a foregone conclusion. But Yanai wanted to make sure that when the time was ripe to enter Tokyo, he'd have the right strategy in place. Simply opening stores in Tokyo wouldn't have the impact he sought. He needed a brand new offering that would cause a stir and serve as a marquee product for months. That's when he learned about a wonderful material made from recycled plastic bottles.

Yanai found his ticket into the Tokyo market with fleece. Soft, lightweight, and exceedingly warm, this new material was just what Uniqlo needed for its winter debut, and Yanai set about deploying fleece in a wide range of products. It was an unqualified success, exceeding all expectations and turning Uniqlo's metropolitan debut into a billion-dollar payoff. Fleece, as was hoped, became a long-seller. Stores were running out of stock within hours of opening, and for the time being, fleece became intimately identified with the Uniqlo brand name. Yanai had come forward with a remarkable combination of patience, strategic planning, and risk-taking intrepidness:

There is always a large factor of chance when it comes to success or failure with a move like that. But the first important thing is to take up the challenge. You may fail many times over. That's fine if it doesn't deter your from picking yourself up, dusting yourself off, and trying again. If you have enough conviction and purpose to carry you through successive attempts, you should have what it takes to eventually succeed.

The Uniqlo Presentation

What largely distinguishes Uniqlo from many of its predecessors and competitors is the way items are displayed and presented in stores. For example, in contrast to many brands that carry nothing but "safe" blacks, whites, and grays during the winter season, Uniqlo stores are bursting with bright colors. The stores are well laid out with wall-to-wall shelves and racks that are easily navigable and color coded. Some have likened it to entering a candy store. The heart races and there's a vibrant ambience that breaks from the staid and monotone atmosphere of most clothing stores.

Another key attribute to the Uniqlo store layout is the intentional placing of women and men's sections on the same floor. This is in contrast to multistory department stores, in which women and men's departments are located on different floors, without exception. Though logical and perhaps convenient, it is not always practical for families trying to shop together. A lot of time is spent in boredom as fathers and children wait for mothers to finish browsing and shopping on their floor. The more time the mothers consume, the less can be spent in the men's or children's departments. Often, families will break for lunch and head home fatigued without seeing the whole store.

Uniqlo's strategy is to have a single spacious floor on which family members can all shop simultaneously in hopes of preventing the "We'll shop for Daddy next time" reflex. It may initially seem unimaginative to have everything spread out over one floor, but this tactic has discernibly boosted Uniqlo sales.

Consumers were in awe of the low prices when Uniqlo first came on the national scene. But the company's advertising campaigns have left an indelible impression on everyone. Uniqlo television ads, in particular, are unlike any by a domestic apparel maker in the past.

The TV commercials are hip, colorful, and captivating. Some have infectious melodies that stick with the viewer, while others consist of only deep breathing and whispering voices. They can be full of kinetic energy, with dozens of happy models walking and dancing past the camera, or a motionless shot of a high-profile celebrity just sitting comfortably.

What Uniqlo commercials succeed most in doing is giving its products a high-end feel. Just when you began to wonder what the commercial is for, the distinctive brand logo appears on screen. The hope is that the viewer's immediate response will be: "What? That model was wearing Uniqlo?" The ad might then end with a bold display of a price: 1,980 yen ($20) for a pair of jeans. All of this has been effective in capturing consumer mindshare for the brand.

Through an onslaught of profile-raising campaigns under a multidirectional approach, be it about price, material, quality or advertising, Yanai succeeded in elevating Fast Retailing (and Uniqlo) to the status of a top-tier company in Japan in just over 10 years. Industry watchers have even begun to speak of Uniqlo as "the company most likely to replace Toyota someday as the first name in Japanese business."

According to "Brand Japan 2009," a Nikkei BP Consulting survey conducted in November 2008, asking general consumers and businesspeople to rate 1,500 brands, Uniqlo came in seventh, ahead of Toyota. In 2007, it was fifty-second. In 2008, it ranked twelfth. By 2009, Uniqlo had emerged as one of the nation's top 10 brands.

And Yanai's company has worked hard to remain in the public eye, with a highly publicized overseas expansion effort, a strong online presence, and a relentless stream of buzz-generating products. So far, by keeping the pressure on and the intensity dialed up, Fast Retailing has earned an overall favorable image among consumers. Quality and price value count most. But Yanai has also worked tirelessly to keep the brand fresh in the national consciousness as he plans his next big move.

A unique online shopping site that rivals the brick-and-mortar experience has proven to be another major key to Uniqlo's success. Uniqlo offers a replete selection of products at the convenience and reduced price points that people have come to expect from internet shopping, complete with internet-only campaigns, weekly events, and various creative promotions to heighten the enjoyment of shopping online. As the company continues to expand the number and size of its brick-and-mortar clothing stores, there are still many people in regional areas that don't have access yet to a physical shop. That's where online shopping can help by building demand organically in less populated areas before locating a store, thereby alleviating the risks of expanding too quickly.

Uniqlo was a relatively early adopter of online clothing retail. By the time most competitors had introduced their websites, Uniqlo could already look back on a wealth of data and know-how and focus its attention on improving the experience. Because it didn't take long for consumers to become internet savvy and choosy about how they wanted to shop online, Uniqlo's lead in the virtual realm has let it concentrate on tailoring its experience to best reflect and augment the brand in a way consistent with efforts in the physical world.

Don't Let Failure Deter You

It is easy to view Fast Retailing as a spirited upstart that achieved near overnight success because of its relative youth and rise from countryside obscurity. But Yanai's rapid expansion drive and innovative marketing strategies have also backfired. Fast Retailing is currently undertaking a second wholehearted attempt at overseas expansion, after having previously entered the UK market with great fanfare only to post large losses.

Fast Retailing is committed to succeeding abroad. The company already ranks seventh among the world's major retail clothing franchises. But Yanai is clearly aiming higher. To stand shoulder to shoulder with the likes of Gap and Limited Brands of the US, and No. 4 Swedish apparel giant, H&M (Hennes & Mauritz), says Yanai: "We need to become a trillion-yen company."

If Uniqlo can exceed the trillion-yen revenue mark, it will find itself within a stone's throw of the top three. For now, the company is still several hundred million short. But one thing is for certain. Yanai is hinging his company's success on becoming a global company. So far, it has shown itself capable of growing through a recession. Operating profit shot up 24 percent to a record 108.6 billion yen for the company's fiscal year ending in August 2009, while group sales climbed 17 percent. This amid what many have called the worst downturn in a century, in which most other retailers are struggling. Tadashi Yanai attributes the success to hit products and high value for cash-strapped consumers. The company expects 2010 to be just as strong if the 30 percent increase in sales for September is any indication. "We're focused on making good clothes," Yanai told reporters. "Consumers appreciate our high-value-added products as they meet their needs."

Overseas Expansion, M&A and Collaboration

If Fast Retailing hopes to reach its stated goal of a trillion yen in group earnings by 2010, and five trillion yen by 2020, the growth will have to come from overseas. Japan still accounts for nearly 90 percent of Uniqlo sales. While the company does operate stores in the US, the UK, France, China, South Korea, Hong Kong, and now Singapore, operating margins are still only about 1.6 billion yen.

A large part of the strategic focus will be on Singapore, where Uniqlo opened its highly publicized Tampines 1 store.

"Becoming number one in Asia is right now the most direct route to global number one," Yanai declared.

Yanai views Singapore as the operational hub and launching point for expanding into Southeast Asia, first, and then to the rest of the continent.

This Asian expansion drive looked to begin kicking into high gear when Fast Retailing announced in early October 2009 its plans to build the largest Uniqlo store in the world in Shanghai in the spring of 2010. The megastore will be positioned as a "global flagship" shop, and will crown the company's efforts to build 100 outlets a year in that market. That same spring will also see the opening of the first Uniqlo outlet in Moscow, an important step toward the company's stated goal of 4,000 outlets around the world.

In Japan, Fast Retailing partnered with the real estate company, Daiwa House Industry, early in its domestic expansion drive. Yanai believes that teaming up with real estate companies with extensive reach in a country gives him the ability to plan his Uniqlo store expansion strategy with greater precision and stability.

So in Singapore, Uniqlo has joined hands with the real estate firm, Wing Tai Holdings, in the hope of gaining ready information on local market conditions and trends. Yet Yanai isn't giving up on his own penchant for learning on his own. He also plans to sell the same winter clothes that Uniqlo does in Japan, despite the year-round tropical climate in Singapore. Some might call it folly. Yanai calls it an experiment:

> Yes, we'll be making use of as much locally sourced information as we can, but since this is our first store in Singapore, we'd like to field-test our products and see for ourselves what sells and what doesn't.

Whether this tack is a reflection of Yanai's confidence or perhaps some hesitation to rely too much on what others say is not clear. Perhaps, the truth lies in both. But one thing it does reveal is Yanai's belief in the value of doubt, forged from the experience of watching the "Uniqlo boom" of 2001 fizzle quickly because of the short attention span of consumers. Yanai has been more careful since to avoid the pitfalls that might make his company just a fleeting phenomenon.

While design quality is high, most Uniqlo clothes fall into the so-called "functional basic" category. This means it is relatively inconspicuous apparel such as underwear or T-shirts that would form only part of an overall ensemble. With the mass support the brand has received so far, there is always the risk that people will suddenly grow tired of, or feel embarrassed by, wearing a lot of the same clothes as their friends and neighbors.

Typically, boom and bust cycles for hit products in Japan are incredibly short. While a product or a celebrity's popularity may soar to astronomical heights quickly, the fall to oblivion is equally precipitous and abrupt. Yanai has felt this firsthand, and it has infused a bit of healthy paranoia in his management philosophy:

> Running a business often feels like building a sandcastle. If you're not vigilant at all times, the tide will suddenly rush in and wash it away. From production to distribution to shop sales, you can't overlook even the smallest problems.

There is another reason overseas expansion is so important for long-term success. Doing so inevitably involves being on the lookout for strategic mergers and acquisitions that will solidify a strong global position. Fast Retailing notably lost a hard-fought battle with Dubai-based investment fund Istithmar in 2007 to acquire the Barneys New York department store, which would have brought the company instantly closer to its trillion-yen goal.

While Uniqlo was forced to withdraw and rethink its strategy, the Barneys experience did give the company some global exposure and recognition. This was the first Japanese clothing brand to really exhibit a willingness and aggressiveness to compete on a global level.

While there are certainly Japanese apparel companies of long-standing international reputations, most focus almost exclusively on manufacturing and sales. Fast Retailing, on the other hand, clearly has its mind set on becoming something larger; a truly global brand that can create new lifestyle values with universal appeal. Uniqlo began to ratchet up this ambition starting at home in 2009.

One of those efforts that drew much attention was the opening of a "megastore" in April 2009 on the west side of the bustling Shinjuku station in Tokyo. The months of buzz circulating about the megastore led to some 400 people lined up outside it on opening day, despite it being a workday. With entry to the store having to be limited, the event attracted media coverage:

> Uniqlo impresses with its ability to constantly maintain and stoke consumer interest in its products with its patented multi-pronged attack on the retail clothing market, this time, by launching its largest store ever in the heart of Shinjuku and fueling the hype by rolling out a new line of high-quality T-shirts that sell for 990 yen (under $10). (*Nihon Keizai* newspaper)

In an attempt to further fire up domestic sales, Uniqlo announced it would expand floor space of its Ginza store one-and-a-half times to exceed 24,500 square feet, putting it in direct competition with the large standalone shops of major foreign rivals such as H&M, Forever 21, and Zara.

When the *Nihon Keizai* newspaper in June released its popular ranking of top products for fiscal year 2008, it named as one of its two "grand champions" something called "Fast Fashion," a playful derivative of the term "fast food" used to describe popular mass-market clothing chains such as Gap, H&M, and Uniqlo.

Fast Retailing also rolled out its "Girls Concept Shop," an exclusively women's apparel outlet that aims to capitalize on the lightning quick sensitivity to changing fashion trends among young women consumers by introducing new product lines ahead of competitors. One extraordinary deal sealed by Yanai was to collaborate with world-renowned German designer Jill Sander on a new collection for autumn 2009. Collaboration such as this is one way outside of M&A activities for Fast Retailing to elevate its brand image, brand equity and name recognition globally, and will be an essential ingredient in putting the company over the one-trillion-yen mark as a group.

Building a planned 200 large-format stores in high consumer-concentrated, metropolitan areas should further accelerate the surge in domestic demand that Uniqlo store openings invariably generate. Particularly in an economic environment where consumers are actively seeking the highest value for their money, Fast Retailing has proven itself adept at offering quality goods at bargain-basement prices. But it will still need to forge ahead with its globalization drive and make some strong acquisitions to make it a viable competitor with global rivals.

The corporate statement for the Fast Retailing Group reads: "Changing clothes. Changing conventional wisdom. Change the world." The mission elucidated under this statement is to create truly great clothing with new and unique value that can bring joy, happiness, and satisfaction to people the world over, and to seek to grow and develop as a company in support of people's lives and in unity with society.

While the touting of Fast Retailing as the company likely "to surpass Toyota as the face of Japanese business" may still be media hyperbole, any major moves Fast Retailing makes are treated as headline news. Indeed, Yanai and Fast Retailing have a flair for drama, but the company has also shown a strong commitment to enhancing value in the second half of its mission statement.

For example, through its All-Product Recycling Initiative, Uniqlo encourages customers to bring clothes they are no longer using to stores for reuse, whether as donations to refugee camps, reprocessing into industrial fiber, or to be recycled and used for electric power generation. In 2008, Uniqlo recycled 1.34 million articles of used clothing, reflecting the company's self-imposed sense of commitment to ensure that value is extended throughout the life of its products, with nothing going to waste.

Summary: The ABCs of Change

Business is always a sustained process of trial-and-error, with limitless failures. Mistakes are a part of business. For every 10 new things you start, nine of them will fail. The business landscape changes with head-spinning speed. The ability to keep pace while ensuring the survival of one's company means one must be constantly willing to reform an entire organization and keep growing. Growth is a company's reason for being.

So wrote the Fast Retailing founder, chairman, president and CEO, Tadashi Yanai, in his book *1 Win, 9 Losses*. What helped make Uniqlo one of Japan's largest companies is a belief in not trying to cover over failure, but rather treating it as a knowledge asset to be exercised in future endeavors. It is a management style that cherishes persistence and a never-say-die attitude.

Whenever Tadashi Yanai is invited to give a lecture, he begins by reminiscing about watching his father sell suits at the family business, Men's Shop Ogori Shoji, in Yamaguchi Prefecture's industrial city of Ube on the Inland Sea coast; and how he grew up believing that this was a business that was not going anywhere. His own personal interest in the business was piqued only after graduating from college and coming home to work at the shop when he struck upon the idea that selling casual clothing would be much more interesting—and rewarding.

So on June 2, 1984 in Hiroshima city, Yanai opened up a casual clothing store called "Unique Clothing Warehouse" (the Fukuromachi store) under the slogan: "a giant warehouse with a constant selection." Yanai had received some important inspiration when he traveled to the US on what amounted to be a fact-finding tour. There, he visited a university cooperative that employed a novel concept of offering low-priced casual clothing to customers in much the same way one purchases magazines. The store was bustling with teens. This became an instrumental influence on Yanai's decision to turn his business into a franchise, and open up more outlets in suburban areas.

From there, it was a process of trial-and-error as he sought to expand his customer base to men and women of all ages, and offer them not only great price value but also high-quality products; the very image of the brand today.

In the process of creating a successful enterprise, Yanai undertook reform challenges. There was the "Takumi Project" aimed at raising product quality; the "ABC Reform" (All Better Change) aimed at changing the company structure to take on more of a customer perspective, and new campaigns to inform people why low-priced but high-quality products sell. With the "Takumi Project," Yanai sent a team of people well versed in Fast Retailing management principles along with seasoned technicians to China to consign production there. They also spoke Chinese, which helped to smooth communications in the guidance process and ensure product quality. The ABC Reform involved having aggressive scouting personnel facilitate the company's shift to a professional management group, emphasizing greater autonomy among individual stores and encouraging greater decision-making independence by store managers.

Yanai has made human resources training a pillar of his company's growth strategy, with plans to launch an in-company business school in 2010 with the aid of the Harvard Business School and Hitotsubashi University. In this way, he follows in the footsteps of great business leaders such as Konosuke Matsushita and Kiichiro

Toyoda, whom he admired and studied as a youth and who did more than create the industrial foundation of modern Japan but also revolutionized the field of business management.

Fast Retailing has so far managed to sustain growth in sales and profits over repeated up-and-down cycles in the economy, and has responded to changes in the business landscape by continually rolling out fresh new products, internalizing a flexibility and culture of constant self-reform, and building a structural framework that allows for necessary changes to be made without fail at great speed. In short, Yanai has never stopped tweaking his management infrastructure. When he switched to a holding-company format in November 2005, he freed his company to concentrate available resources on overseas apparel development.

Yanai brought Uniqlo to the UK in 2001, but soon realized he did so without enough due diligence and without truly establishing sufficient store management know-how. As a result, the company struggled and had to pull back some. But that proved an important lesson for the company's strategy for the Chinese market, where it was decided the next solid foundation would be built, one store at a time. That more deliberate style has proven sound so far, and seems to have put Uniqlo's global expansion effort on a solid track.

When Tadashi Yanai inherited the keys to his father's business, he was faced for the first time in his life with questions to which he had previously given only scant attention: "What is a good company? What makes a good business?" One by one, he began writing down management principles of his own. One of the most important among them was: "Respond to the wishes of customers, and manage your business to generate more." Yanai's success so far and his bid to make Fast Retailing a global leading company rest on continuing this effort indefinitely.

Principal Ideas of Tadashi Yanai

- Don't cover over failure, but treat it as a knowledge asset.
- Respond to customers' wishes and manage your business to generate more.
- Study, learn and keep the ideas coming. That's the joy of business.

Fast Retailing Co., Ltd.

Established: May 1, 1963
Tadashi Yanai, President and CEO
Head office: 717-1, Sayama, Yamaguchi City
http://www.fastretailing.com/eng
Capital: 10,200 million yen (year ending August 2009)
Consolidated sales: 685,043 million yen
Consolidated operating profit: 108,639 million yen
Consolidated net profit: 49,797 million yen
Employees: 8,054

8

GROWING IN A WORLD
OF CHANGE

Kazuyasu Kato
President and CEO
Kirin Holdings Co., Ltd.

Born November 1944. Shizuoka Prefecture. Graduated from Keio University's Faculty of Business and Commerce in March 1968, and joined the Kirin Beer Company in April. Held posts as general manager for the Hokkaido Sales Head Office (1997–2000), general manager of Kyushu Sales Head Office (2000–01), general manager of sales and marketing, later adding the title managing director of Kirin Holdings Company, then president and COO (2006). Named president and CEO of Kirin Holdings in July 2007.

A Fascination with German Beer

Kirin Beer was established in 1907 when it took over operations of the Japan Brewery Company. The Japan Brewery Company was located on the former site of the Spring Valley Brewery Company, founded by a Norwegian-born American, William Copeland, who had built an ale and lager beer brewery in Yokohama.

Copeland arrived in Japan already trained in beer-brewing techniques, and decided he wanted to bring great ale and lager to the expatriate community. Copeland was a capable brewer who was able to make some innovations to traditional brewing methods he had learned, including applying French scientist and biologist Louis Pasteur's low-temperature disinfection method—pasteurization.

Spring Valley Brewery's reputation grew primarily through word of mouth, winning the appreciative support of its intended target. So popular was the brand that Copeland even began exporting his products overseas, particularly to other Asian destinations as Shanghai, Hong Kong, and Vietnam.

Other breweries sprung up in Yokohama around that time, one before and one after Spring Valley's emergence, so there was no scarcity of competition. For the next 14 years, Spring Valley had to fight for every inch of market share.

But Copeland's contribution to Japanese industry was pervasive. He enthusiastically took on many young Japanese apprentices, unsparingly sharing with them all of his technical expertise and insights, and even did a good business selling ingredients and equipment to aspiring brewers.

Although Spring Valley had eventually disappeared, The Japan Brewery Company shared its primary objective of brewing authentic German beer. Veteran German brewmasters were recruited and the most advanced equipment and steaming systems of the time were acquired, all under the mantra of providing Japanese consumers with the most authentic quality and satisfying taste possible. This mastercraftsperson approach to authenticity and quality has been enthusiastically passed on through generations of brewers at Kirin Beer.

Much of the world can recognize the Kirin beer label with its distinctive logo of the "Kirin" (*Qilin*), a mythical dragon-like beast from Chinese lore said to feed only on vegetation and loathe the destruction of life. The peaceful creature was said to live for a thousand years.

Demand for beer grew rapidly amid Japan's strong economy following its victory in the Sino-Japanese War of 1894–95. But the enactment of a heavy beer tax law in 1901 had the effect of weeding out many of the small- and medium-sized breweries, leading to cutthroat price wars and competition for market share among the biggest players. By the time the dust had settled, there was one dominant player, The DaiNippon Beer Company, formed through the union of three other breweries: Sapporo Beer Co., Japan Brewery, Ltd., (Yebisu Beer's brewing company), and Osaka Breweries, Ltd. (forerunner to Asahi Beer Co.). The union took place as a way to end the bloodshed, but it also gave birth to a monolithic beer company commanding a 70 percent share of the market.

A worthy rival was needed. So in February 1907, the Japan Brewery Company, with the capital and resource help of major industrialists such as Hisaya Iwasaki of the Mitsubishi conglomerate, reformed as the Kirin Brewery Company.

The singular pursuit of authentic German beer quality remained the primary mission, however, and beer continued to be brewed with imported ingredients under German brewmaster supervision. The public's perception of Kirin as a producer of "real" German beer helped it quickly close the lead that DaiNippon Beer Company had gained in the time since its merger. Workers at Kirin beamed with confidence that they could keep eating into their rival's market share. But then, World War II broke out and all beer manufacturing went into hiatus.

A shortage of raw materials kept beer production low after the war, giving Kirin little opportunity to gain ground on DaiNippon. What's more, the US-led allied occupation command, GHQ, had placed restrictions on the production of beer. Kirin had to find a way to survive, so it turned to earning whatever revenue it could by brewing soy sauce and renting out empty warehouses.

Kirin managers deserve great credit for keeping the company viable and its facilities in working order for the next decade. For no sooner had the restrictions on beer production been lifted in 1954 when Kirin instantly jumped out in front of its prewar rivals and catapulted itself into the nation's biggest beer producer, a position the company would hold for the next 45 years.

Through periods of heavy competition, war, and regulation, Kirin stayed true to its simply articulated mission of brewing high-quality, German-style beer; a commitment that has continually made the brewer the industry's standard bearer, earning the unwavering trust of generations of consumers while forcing its competitors to strive for equal levels of excellence.

Mining Consumer Demand

One of Kirin's biggest reform efforts has been the introduction and evolution of "Kirinology," an information-sharing system deployed throughout the group's infrastructure to mine, compile, and analyze information from the field (*genba*) quickly, and by doing so, rapidly ascertain changing market conditions.

The Kirinology system was launched in the summer of 2003 to disseminate freshly gathered information to all vital bases around the country. But the initial reception to the system was mixed, as people encountered many difficulties in using what was a proprietary in-house system.

The burden on system operators to collect as much information as possible and not let a shred of potentially useful data go undetected proved initially onerous and impractical. The Kirinology project was ambitious to begin with, so it would take several years of adjustments before it began to live up to its billing as a dynamic information-mining and sharing system for the twenty-first century. The myriad varieties of information the system was supposed to draw up included normative indications of exactly what consumers were feeling and desiring at a particular time, and what consumer trends were beginning to take shape in different regions.

The results have been nothing short of revolutionary. Implementation of Kirinology in the development and marketing of new products enabled Kirin to regain its crown as top market shareholder for most of fiscal 2006, after "languishing" in second place for six years.

Kirin also welcomed a gutsy new president in Kazuyasu Kato in 2006, who truly embodied the company's renewed sense of leadership for a new age and from the start has displayed a great eagerness to convert the company's newfound momentum into growth.

> Kirinology has achieved much more than we expected, whether you're talking about new types of point-of-purchase advertisements we've put up in retail stores, or temporary sales booths that recreate the atmosphere of our television commercials; all of these things have helped boost sales because they are the result of consumer voices being heard all the way through the company. Conversely, each "successful case" is immediately conveyed to all points around the country as sort of a best practice reference, which can then be emulated, adapted or disseminated across the organization.

From Hokkaido to Kyushu, Kato says there are close to 100 exchanges of practical information being pushed across the company daily. Ideas and practices that prove effective or beneficial in some way are rapidly absorbed and introduced, while things that don't work instantly serve as useful lessons as well. People in the field have come to realize that they have tremendous resources at their disposal and the strength of the whole company behind them.

The average Japanese consumer may not have noticed it yet, but Kato also carried this spirit of group unity to the company logo, adopting the Kirin logo for all group companies to better position the Kirin brand as a management asset. Before this move, there had been about a half-dozen different logos used for various divisions. By unifying the group under one logo, the company can look to manage the brand more consistently and thoroughly, while also reserving the famous Kirin symbol exclusively for beer products.

The Kirin logo is managed by Kirin Holdings, under a licensing system similar to that used by the private railway company and department store chain, Tokyu Corporation, in which logo usage fees are set to a fixed scale commensurate with business sales volume.

In Search of New, Diverse Opportunities

What sets the new Kirin apart from the old is a proactive approach to diversification around its core beer products. Whereas in the past this may have come about more through necessity and almost as a distraction from the company's abiding passion to beer, today, "diversification" is a central pillar of the company's long-term management vision.

Under Kirin Holdings, the group has a pharmaceutical division headlined by specialty pharma company called Kyowa Hakko Kirin, and a flower seed business through Kirin Agribio Company. Both companies have a strong global composition. Beer and other spirits continue to be produced and sold through Kirin's alcohol beverages division, companies such as Kirin Brewery Company and Lion Nathan Ltd., while softdrinks and fruit juices are handled by its beverage divisions, such as Kirin Beverage and National Foods Limited, all capitalizing on accumulated know-how, equipment, and human resources.

Sailing into uncharted commercial waters outside of one's traditional comfort zone has mandated not only the cultivation of a new corporate image, but also internal structural and systemic changes. Indeed, diversification and expansion are the only options when growth in a foundation business can no longer be expected, or when future growth in a foundation business can no longer yield revenues substantial enough to sustain a company of Kirin's size and stature.

In such situations, there is greater risk to inaction than action; and a well-laid overt strategy to diversify can allow a company to look beyond the short-term hurdles of each new venture.

Coupled with the need to broaden its business segment horizons is an imperative to expand globally. Ever since "globalization" became the buzzword for success in Japan in the late 1980s, corporate boardrooms across the country have been scampering to reorganize themselves and craft new long-term targets and strategies in a global context. It means Japanese companies need to make themselves universally understood, whether to consumers in the form of their product offerings, or to investors and shareholders in the form of clearly stated philosophies and financial reportage.

This takes concrete shape in a set of four major values and action stances entitled the "Kirin Way," beginning with "striving to understand the customer better than any competitor, (and) remembering the importance of communication . . ." While the first rule of business in Japan has long been to treat the customer as god, customer satisfaction in today's highly diversified, specialized and globalized world increasingly requires less "deference to" the customer himself or herself and more "knowledge of" the customer's every need. In this sense, the dynamic of the traditional customer–client relationship is being altered, from one of infallible master and subject, to cooperative partners. If your customer is an unknowable god, then you must place yourself at his or her beck and call when he or she makes demands. But if your customer is an intimate friend, then you're probably already meeting his or her demands even before they are made.

The Kirin Way raises the relentless pursuit of quality as its second value, through constant improvements in technology and processes, and thorough attention to detail. This has been most emphatically shown in Kirin's constant endeavor to improve its chilling technologies and ensure "freshness" as the life of beer.

The third value is innovation; fostering the free-thinking spirit and vision necessary for generating new ideas. When beer sales were slumping in the early 1990s, the beer industry saved itself with the invention of *happo-shu*, a low-malt beer or sparkling spirit cheaper than beer because of a lower rate of taxation. The invention of whole new beverage categories has become *de rigueur* for beer brands hoping to supplant dwindling beer consumption with new revenue streams; the most recent trend being nonalcoholic beverages that mimic beer in taste without the inebriating effects. Without a constant supply of fresh new ideas to meet, or better yet, pre-empt changes in consumer demand, Kirin and other breweries would gradually find themselves serving what amounts to only a niche market.

The last value in the Kirin Way is "Integrity—Maintaining a fair-minded and earnest stance toward all business activities." It is the value that workers at Kirin must remain most vigilant about upholding at all times.

As do all strong and dynamic companies that have a knack for survival, Kirin views difficult times as the best opportunity to make bold moves. For Kirin, that means moving ahead with growth in areas outside its primary beer division, such as (nonalcoholic) beverages, food products, and pharmaceuticals; all three of which are posting stable growth. Kirin's strategy is to build up these businesses first domestically.

In contrast to over trillion yen in alcoholic beverage revenues, Kirin's pharmaceutical division is a 170 billion-yen business, while nonalcoholic beverages earn about 710 billion yen. Overseas alcohol and food has grown into a lucrative multibillion-dollar business for Kirin. Though quantitatively falling far below alcoholic beverages, all ancillary businesses are growing. Kirin is experiencing even stronger growth in newer endeavors, such as health and functional foods, seasonings, and agribio, to name a few.

There is always room for growth in one's core business, even if it doesn't promise double-digit returns. In December 2006, Kirin Holdings brought winemaker Mercian into its group in a capital and business alliance aimed at building on mutual strengths and strengthening weaknesses. Kirin was not particularly strong in wine, so that business is centered on Mercian while Kirin handles the popular *shochu* distilled spirits and ready-to-drink mixed alcoholic beverages.

The same year, Kirin purchased major pharma company Kyowa Hakko. Under Kazuyasu Kato, strategic acquisitions and alliances do offer instant growth. But the key to Kirin's long-term growth remains a dedication to development of attractive new products.

One new nonalcoholic beverage product that has earned overwhelming support from women in their 20s to 30s is a softdrink series called "The World's Kitchen." Kirin researchers have been going into household kitchens around the world to see what kind of traditional and popular concoctions homemakers in various countries and regions make; using those recipes as inspiration for creating a unique and exotic new lineup of softdrinks focusing on constituent ingredients. The drink names and packaging are as novel as the drinks themselves, conveying less of a beverage image than one of a drinkable food entree. The series intentionally evokes home-cooked warmth such as peach compote, based on a dessert recipe by homemakers in the Hungarian countryside, or a sparkling soda that mimics the taste of a Cuban *mojito*.

In this way, Kazuyasu Kato is bringing a revolutionary style of leadership to a company traditionally known for its no-debt pruden-tism. Instead, he is instilling a culture of risk-taking activism, com-plete with dramatic M&As and new sector forays, to ensure that Kirin remains viable and growing long after beer has become simply one among many integral parts of its business. In its "identity state-ment," the Kirin Group defines itself as "focused on people, nature, and craftsmanship to redefine the joy of food and health."

Be Thorough and Persistent in Getting Results

Kazuyasu Kato is the first to admit there's a lot to be done:

> With beer, I think objectives are clear. Amid this global reces-sion, and the shrinking that has been going on in this industry for some years now, our performance in relative terms has been strong. That said, the recession is sure to continue for a while and hard battles will be fought. So it is imperative that we continue to give the consumer products that they will openly embrace and be the best in that sphere.
>
> For other alcoholic beverages such as *shochu* and *chuhai* (popular Japanese spirits distilled from a variety of ingredients), there is much we could do. For example, our Kirin Chu-hai Hyoketsu product sold well. But we still needed to aim much higher, and I won't deny we came up a little short on effort. Our overall strategy for the *shochu* business needs to be clari-fied, such as whether we can conceivably raise consumer sup-port in that category. That's something I'd like to have concerted discussions about going forward. We need to be aggressively positioned in everything.

One of the aggressive positions Kirin took in 2009 was to strengthen its Western spirits business, establishing a joint partnership with London-based Diageo PLC. Diageo products include Guinness, Johnnie Walker Scotch whisky, and Smirnoff Ice alcoholic beverages.

Western spirits are a very important segment to Kirin. But past efforts haven't resulted in significant growth in that business.

The partnership with Diageo aims to bolster Japanese consumer access to many world-renowned alcoholic beverage brands.

The resulting company, Diageo Kirin Co., with 51 to 49 percent ownership by Diageo and Kirin, respectively, makes it easier to distribute Diageo's major brands by cutting out a lot of intermediaries for such highly recognized products such as Johnnie Walker whisky, Gordon's gin, Guinness, Smirnoff vodka, and Baileys rum among many others.

The April 2009 release of "Kirin Free" augurs well for the establish-ment of a new segment for Kirin, which shipped 340,000 cases of the nonalcoholic beverage in the first month, and looks to exceed annual sales projections of 630,000 cases by the end of only the second month. Produced under Kirin's safety and environment program, Kirin Free has been billed as a beer-flavored beverage you can safely drink before driving. It is said to recreate the taste and fragrance of beer at a level far beyond conventional "near beer" beverages or even low-alcohol imitations. While drunk-driving acci-dents in Japan have dropped to one-fifth the number of 10 years ago, the hope is that popularity of products like these will contribute to further decreases.

Viewed as a technological coup, the product was developed by members from both beer and *chuhai* divisions (*chuhai* being *shochu* flavored with fruit or soda) as the *chuhai* division boasts Kirin's leading flavoring experts.

Kirin marketers made sure to emphasize the complete nonalco-holic content of the drink, adding a "0.00" on the label where alcoholic content is usually designated. Consumers were consulted or took active part in every stage of development from taste-testing surveys and consumer interviews to establishing a product name and concept. Package design was even conducted over the internet. It had to be a consumer-driven product.

The biggest challenge for Kirin and Kazuyasu Kato going for-ward may be how to preserve and extend the strong reputation and tradition that Kirin has built as a beer brand while also reinvent-ing Kirin as a new age brand that doesn't *just* make beer. When asked what kind of leadership will be required to reconcile these two forces and ensure Kirin's growth into a top-tier global company for years to come, Kato's response was true to form: "Leaders who take clear action."

Summary: From Brewery to Food Giant

Kirin Beer established slightly bitter-tasting German-style lager as the most popular type of beer in Japan. For nearly three-quarters of a century and practically all of commercial beer-brewing history in Japan, Kirin ruled the industry.

Then in 1987, Kirin would find itself suddenly upended by a perennial junior rival, Asahi Beer, with a single product called "Super Dry," a very dry lager that quickly became the nation's beer of choice. Asahi steadily gained on both Kirin and Sapporo Breweries, until finally usurping the crown from Kirin in 2001 as the nation's number one brewery in volume sales. The age of two beer powerhouses slugging it out for market leadership had begun.

But the pie they fought over was shrinking fast, because of diversifying demand and a shrinking population. They were two large fish in an evaporating pond, and something had to change.

As soon as Kazuyasu Kato assumed the top position at Kirin in March 2006, he launched a strong M&A initiative at home and abroad, capped by the July 2009 announcement that Kirin and Suntory Holdings would merge, bringing two of the country's leading beer and beverage companies under one roof. The merger between Kirin and Suntory will put some distance between them and the current beer-market leader, Asahi Breweries, with roughly 50 percent to Asahi's 38 percent, and is also likely to fuel a rapid realignment in the country's food industry overall. Some analysts point to the potential trouble of merging a privately held firm, Suntory, with a listed one, Kirin. But it should also lead to greater efficiencies in procurement and production, giving the new company the increased margins it will need to acquire overseas rival firms and survive domestic market contraction.

Asahi, too, has pursued an active expansion and diversification drive that includes acquisitions of domestic and foreign food concerns. But Kirin Holdings does harbor distinct advantages and skills when it comes to large-scale organizational initiatives as one of close to 400 companies across 30 sectors that come under Mitsubishi Group ownership. The main aim of the merger, however, is to generate increasingly higher revenues from overseas.

Still, even if one was to combine the earnings of Kirin's pharmaceuticals and medical supply maker Kyowa Hakko, and overseas beverage and food holdings, they still wouldn't even amount to half of the trillion yen Kirin earns (with Mercian) in the domestic alcoholic beverage market. Yet Kirin is determined to fortify its core beer business with a high-powered strategy to become a diversified global conglomerate and leading food products purveyor in Asia and Oceania. "The Day Kirin Transcends Beer" ran a headline in the *Nikkei Business* magazine of March 3, 2008.

The change toward a diversified strategy actually began in 2001 with company president Koichiro Aramaki, a Tokyo University agriculture department graduate who rose through the ranks of the company in the pharmaceutical, not beverage, division. Aramaki believed that Kirin must fashion a vision that looks much further into the future than just three years, and pointed to the need to diagnose and harness the collective power of the Kirin group for greater integration focused on customers and quality. Aramaki announced these reforms in a "New Kirin Declaration," in which he characterized the company's strength as rooted firmly in "beer" and "fermentation-based technologies," and that a replete array of alcoholic beverages, nonalcoholic beverages, food products, and pharmaceutical products would arm Kirin with the strength to expand overseas while reinforcing domestic foundations at home. To accomplish all of this, Kirin would need to switch to a holding-company structure.

Kazuyasu Kato succeeded Aramaki as Kirin president in 2006. Although he came up through the company's alcoholic beverage division, he immediately sought to put the company's abundant cash reserves to work under an aggressive, long-term investment strategy. Kirin purchased a large equity stake in Mercian, and merged its pharmaceutical arm with Kyowa Hakko to become the Kyowa Hakko Kirin Co. Moreover, it went on the hunt for quality acquisitions in Asia and Oceania, beginning in Australia with the country's largest dairy product and beverage maker, National Foods, then snapping up second-largest player, Dairy Farmers, and increasing its stake in Australia's second largest beer maker, Lion Nathan, before moving to the Philippines to raise its ownership of San Miguel Brewery Inc. to 48 percent, the beer unit of the Philippines' largest food company.

In the three-plus years since 2006, Kirin has plunked down more than a trillion yen on acquisitions. The announcement of Kirin's plan to merge with Suntory prompted a Kirin managing director, Yoshiharu Furumoto to comment: "We have now acquired most of the companies we should be purchasing." Kato himself has repeatedly said that growth on one's own has its limits, and that raising revenues through such mergers will give Kirin the strength to accelerate overseas expansion drive. If the Kirin–Suntory merger goes through (it was still in discussion at the time of this book's publishing), it will create a beverage behemoth with 3.82 trillion yen in sales, overtaking Anheuser-Busch InBev of Belgium as world's top brewer, as well as the Coca-Cola Co. of the US as top beverage producer, and catapult the new entity into the ranks of the top five general food companies in the world.

All this activity would have struck many as surprising just a few years ago, since Kirin had long been known for a conservative style of management, much like the Mitsubishi Group to which it belongs. Kirin prided itself on carrying very low debt throughout its history. In the 1970s, Kirin reached and maintained roughly a 64 percent share of the domestic beer market.

But in the 1980s, perennial second-fiddle rival, Asahi Beer, finally came out from under Kirin's shadow with its mega-hit product, Super Dry, which seemed to cast Asahi as on top of changing consumer tastes in Japan. Kirin failed to provide an effective counterattack, and eventually fell to second place behind Asahi in its foundation beer business. Kazuyasu Kato is hoping that a renewed and aggressive Kirin, one that is broader in scope and more united in effort, can capitalize on Mitsubishi Group's strength of "long-term strategic thinking" and "organization" and become to the world what it had been to Japan for a century: a leader.

Principal Ideas of Kazuyasu Kato

- Strive to understand the customer better than any of your competitors.
- Don't sit on your core strengths, but use them as a force of change and new growth.
- We must promote a culture that encourages expansion, risk-taking, and diversification.

Kirin Holdings Co., Ltd.

Established: February 23, 1907 (Kirin Brewery Company)

Kazuyasu Kato, President and CEO

Head office: 2-10-1, Shinkawa, Chuo-ku, Tokyo

http://www.kirin.co.jp/english/

Capital: 102,000 million yen (year ending December 2008)

Consolidated sales: 2,303,569 million yen

Consolidated operating profit: 145,977 million yen

Consolidated net profit: 80,182 million yen

Employees: 36,554

9

REVIVING THE ENGINE OF
JAPAN INC.

Akio Mimura
Representative Director and Chairman
Nippon Steel Corp.

Born November 1940 in Gunma Prefecture. Graduated from Tokyo University's Faculty of Economics in March 1963. Joined Fuji Iron & Steel Co. (now Nippon Steel) in April. Became representative director and president in 2003, then chairman in 2008. Served as the eleventh chairman of the Japan Iron & Steel Federation from 2003 to 2006. Also vice chairman of the Japan Business Federation from 2005 to 2009, and chairman of the Central Council for Education under the Japanese Ministry of Education, Culture, Sports, Science, and Technology. Currently a member of the National Council on Economic and Fiscal Policy.

Leadership Learned through Volleyball

"As steel goes, so goes the country."

If there's anyone in Japan who believes in the continued relevance of this often-repeated quote from Japan's heady industrial past, it would have to be former Nippon Steel Corporation chairman, Akio Mimura, who capitalized on a rising China to orchestrate a resurgence of his company's core business early in the twenty-first century.

Mimura was born in a country town in Gunma Prefecture just outside the Tokyo metropolitan area, and was said to have walked the proverbial five miles in the snow to kindergarten as a child. When he was named captain of his school's volleyball team in his second year of middle school, it awakened in him a passion for competition and leadership. After guiding his school to a third place finish in the prefectural championship tournament, Mimura set his sights on getting a higher education.

Mimura gained entry to the country's top university, Tokyo University, and put himself through college with what he could earn as a home tutor. When he could manage it, he sent money home. Though regarded by his classmates as extremely studious, Mimura continued to play volleyball. Between studies, sports, and part-time work, his time was always occupied.

When in his third year Mimura's thoughts turned to a career, he knew that all the struggle and sacrifice was about to pay off. For graduating from the prestigious Tokyo University all but guaranteed he'd have the pick of the lot among the country's top companies. But Mimura's mind worked differently from those of most of his peers:

> I figured if I had a choice, I would prefer to join a company that was not first in its field. That way, I'd have something to shoot for. I had enough ambition for two people at the time. I truly wanted to feel like I was contributing to Japan's economic development.

When enrolled in a college class called "The Economics of Steel," Mimura had the opportunity to visit NKK Steel (now JFE Steel Corp.), an industrial powerhouse and shipbuilder during World War II. What Mimura saw there made his heart race with excitement. Enthralled by the sheer force and dynamism of an ironworks factory, Mimura had found his calling. As soon as he graduated from Tokyo University, Mimura joined Fuji Iron & Steel (now Nippon Steel) and began to live and breathe steel.

Usiminas: Japan's Brazilian Advantage

At a press club interview held in December 2007, Mimura was queried by a reporter about what Nippon Steel's strategy was amid the global realignment taking place in the industry.

"Raising demand for high-grade steel is a pressing one," Mimura replied. "Here at home, we would like to increase the sizes of our blast furnaces at Kimitsu and Yawata Works. Oh, and by the way, we have a plan to build the largest furnace in the world at Usiminas in Brazil."

Usiminas can shed light on both the path that Japanese steel has traveled thus far as well as on where it is going.

Cooperation between Japan and Brazil in steel dates back to 1958 when the two countries launched Usinas Sederurgicas de Minas Gerais S.A. (Usiminas for short) as a jointly financed steel works.

The central player on the Japanese side at the time was Yawata Steel Works (now a part of Nippon Steel). Brazil was still dependent on agriculture as its primary industry. But unlike Japan, it was a country rich in natural resources. What it lacked was technical know-how, equipment, and sufficient capital to develop its own steel industry. Building a large-scale steel factory was a tall order, but one with promising dividends.

Under president Juscelino Kubitschek, the Brazilian government announced an enormous five-year economic development plan and public works program, passing new laws and offering incentives to attract private investment that could spearhead an aggressive import-substitution industrialization policy. The Japanese government was canvassed to take part in laying the groundwork for establishing a Brazilian steel works with the full cooperation of Japanese steelmakers. The Usiminas Steel Works project involved more than construction. It was also an urbanization plan that included the building of housing and cultural facilities.

Eight residential districts rose around the factory, including more than 10 social gathering clubs and various amusement facilities in the hope of keeping workers and residents satisfied. The infrastructure included a hospital to serve not just factory personnel but also residents in surrounding communities. Local schools were built and managed by Usiminas personnel. But these, too, were open to the general public. In short, it was a massive community planning project to be built and developed together with local residents and centered around a burgeoning steel industry, namely Usiminas.

Despite this long history, and Nippon Steel being a major shareholder in Ushiminas through its subsidiary investment firm, Nippon Usiminas, the company had not actively sought to build on this relationship until quite recently, when Brazil emerged as one of the world's most promising markets together with Russia, India, and China.

Moreover, the world's top steelmaker, the ArcelorMittal Group of India, was rumored to be considering a possible takeover of

Usiminas. The Japanese steel industry had been the first to enter into a partnership with Brazil, helping to seed a steel industry long before any other country. Nippon Steel decided it was time to bolster its interests in the region, and in 2006 increased its holdings in Nippon Usiminas from 14.4 percent to 50.9 percent, formally announcing Nippon Usiminas as a consolidated subsidiary, with contributions now to show up in Nippon Steel's accounting books. It was a show of Nippon Steel group's ambition to acquire more foreign holdings amid global consolidation of the industry.

By putting Nippon Usiminas under its control and improving business performance, Nippon Steel could orchestrate a rise in Usiminas' share value and make it difficult for Mittal to consider a takeover. Although Nippon Steel trails only Mittal in steel production, Mittal produces three times the tonnage of Nippon Steel.

Usiminas enjoys a virtual monopoly in Brazil for galvanized steel sheets used in shipbuilding and automobiles and Nippon Steel has been jointly manufacturing galvanized steel sheets called UNIGAL with Usiminas since 1999. The steel sheeting has been praised for its technical strength.

Before the global economic downturn of 2008, Brazil had been receiving great attention as one of the world's most promising regions of economic growth; a BRIC nation, standing for Brazil, Russia, India and China. This growth prompted increased activity in Brazil by Japanese automakers, which in turn boosted demand for steel and, particularly, automotive galvanized steel sheets.

Better Troubleshooting and Quick Recovery

Steel has long been a leading bellwether for describing the state of a nation's economy, and Japan is no exception. But for nearly a generation, from the 1980s into the 1990s, the price and supply of steel plummeted, prompting people to describe it as a "sunset industry:"

> Things were really tough. Really tough. We were forced to slash costs by some 460 billion yen. That's not something you can do overnight. If we could, we'd have done it already. Yet we had to find places to cut costs somewhere, and quickly.

Akio Mimura was handed the unenviable task of holding a cost-cutting conference and uttering the most horrific word in the postbubble years of the Japanese economy: "restructuring."

The approach we decided to take involved, first, a lot of deliberation and debate to weigh our options carefully and thoroughly. But once a conclusion was reached, we would act swiftly, without remorse. We've found that if discussions are thorough and inclusive enough, taking action is often the easy part. Still, we decided to close four furnaces, reducing domestic capacity from 13 to nine plants. The impact was felt hard in those communities as well as in the lives of shed workers and their families. But it had to be done.

For Nippon Steel, this was an unprecedented level of reform, and pain, to endure. The worst part of it all was that no amount of cost cutting could bring them within view of the light at the end of the tunnel.

"It was agonizing," recalls Mimura. "But we remained confident of the future. It couldn't last forever. The conditions that shaped results in one year are invariably different in the next year. The hardships we were facing were also being felt most everywhere else. So we knew we had the wherewithal to overcome this crisis, and many more crises to come. We had faith that we would rise again."

Nippon Steel had to make what Mimura calls both "scary choices and more focused efforts." But in the end, the company learned that it was certainly capable of riding out an unprecedented storm and arriving on new shores with its spirit intact.

The Future of Steel

Mimura stepped down in the spring of 2008 to be succeeded by Shoji Muneoka, who immediately vowed to continue along the path that his predecessor had paved for him.

"My top priority is to ensure that we position ourselves as a global player," he proclaimed.

Unfortunately, only six months into his tenure, Muneoka would see demand for steel once again stagnate with the onset of the global slowdown in the fall of 2008. But because the future for the industry had looked exceedingly rosy upon entering the recession, Muneoka believes it won't take too long before seeing a recovery, at least to levels equal to the first half of 2008 before the slowdown:

True, output is only about 50 percent of total capacity, so I won't deny times right now are tough. But if signs of a gradual recovery in the automotive electronics market prove real, and lead to recovery among large commercial manufacturers, we should return to at least 70 percent of production capability in the near future.

While the bad timing of Muneoka's appointment to the company's top slot should be chalked up to force majeure—the recession struck amid Nippon Steel enjoying rising demand for steel from China—the new boss inherited another challenge that was foreseeable.

Specifically, it had to do with the medium-term targets announced by the Prime Minister Cabinet's Global Warming Prevention Headquarters for reducing greenhouse gas emissions. According to an April 2009 report published by the Ministry of Economic, Trade, and Industry and Ministry of the Environment, Nippon Steel topped the list of corporate greenhouse gas emitters in fiscal 2007 at 63.05 million tons.

The company would have liked nothing more than to raise production to meet the increased demand, but it must do so while holding down emissions. Developing technology that can sharply reduce emissions in the iron-manufacturing process will prove costly, even as it promises to put the company in a strong position vis-a-vis all other competitors going forward.

"Prime Minister Hatoyama at the launch of his cabinet announced a national CO_2 reduction target of 25 percent from 1990 levels by 2020, a mark that Muneoka said would be extremely tough to hit even for a company with world-class technological levels like Nippon Steel.

At the World Steel Association in December 2008, Muneoka issued the dour prediction that global steel demand would decelerate, due of course to the global recession. Rising crude oil prices had already signaled a slowdown in steel production, only to receive a knockout blow when the global financial crisis hit:

The current global economic downturn quickly offset the unprecedented speed of growth the industry had been experiencing over the past few years prior with growth humming at a scintillating 7 percent per annum. I guess it was too good to last. Now we'd be happy with just a fraction of that growth. Anything over 5 percent just seems unrealistic.

Among colleagues at the New York conference, Mimura projected the gloomiest outlook for the industry with recovery at two-to-three years down the road. But there are structural advantages in place for Nippon Steel that serve to brighten the edges of that forecast.

"Over 40 percent of goods manufactured in Japan are being exported to developing countries," Muneoka notes. "This is a markedly higher percentage than exports by other advanced nations to those same markets. For Nippon Steel, this has translated into a relatively strong cash position. So we do not plan to downgrade our capital investment plans any time soon. There's no doubt that we've entered a period with some struggles ahead. But it is particularly in such times that we have to move ahead with necessary reforms and lay the groundwork that will put us in great stead in the future."

Muneoka was speaking about Japanese industry in general, where on a comparative basis globally, many Japanese firms have entered the global recession already having done most of the heavy lifting to rationalize and refocus their operations, and now have the strong cash reserves to make strategic acquisitions that their overseas rivals cannot.

Looking at the world as a whole, the steel industry is in a period of grand realignment and consolidation. Even compared to a decade ago, you'd be hard pressed to find a large steel company that isn't involved in some kind of M&A strategy or alliance. I think this large wave of structural change was actually brought on by an earlier crisis—the Asian financial crisis that came out of Thailand in 1997.

Indeed, before the global financial recession, Nippon Steel was in talks to partner with Mittal Steel to expand automotive steel production in North America. The world's number one and two steel companies also have joint ventures in high-end automotive sheet steel production that include technology sharing and investment in expanded capacity. Nippon Steel is also in negotiations with India's Tata Steel to make steel for automobiles in India's burgeoning market. Nippon Steel has already had a technical alliance with Tata Steel since 2002, helping to build steel mills in the country. But this added collaboration would enable Nippon Steel to produce steel directly for use in Japanese cars (Toyota Motor Corp. and Suzuki Motor Corp.) being manufactured in one of the world's fastest-growing and largest markets. Nippon Steel already makes automotive steel in Brazil and China.

The initiative is currently only targeted at high-tension steel sheets produced at facilities we jointly operate with Tata. But we hope this will open the door for more value-added steel that we produce as well. We expect great things in India, but in terms of market presence, partnerships and infrastructure, we've still got a lot of work to do.

If the Japanese steel industry is going to continue to grow and not become a "sunset industry" as once predicted, it'll need to do so through increased demand for high-grade, highly functional steel, such as that used in auto bodies, hybrid car motors, and ships—qualities such as superior electrical conductivity, flexibility and strength, advanced anticorrosive properties, and durability under extreme pressure. So it is important that we be able to produce high-quality steel at just the right time and volume that is demanded. Oversupply in today's global economic environment is the kiss of death. You need to be able to quickly adjust for and rectify any areas of overcapacity. But this is not confined to times of recession. No matter how much you may want to expand, overproduction hurts performance. So it's a fine balancing act. Having just the right capacity and a great sense of timing will secure future success, at home and in the world.

China's rapid economic and industrial growth in recent years was the real linchpin for Nippon Steel's resurgence. But Nippon Steel does wield world-class technology and quality levels. By bringing Usiminas in Brazil closer to the fold, Nippon Steel has also shown that it is willing and able to hold its own under increasingly global competitive pressures. But those pressures should continue to mount, and so too will Nippon Steel's efforts to reshape its destiny.

Summary: Patient Management, Constant Innovation

Nippon Steel has long shouldered much of the weight of and responsibility for Japan's industrial growth. The Meiji Restoration of 1868 put in place a modern, outward-looking government in Japan that quickly adopted an industrialization policy of playing catchup to the West by encouraging the development of important domestic industries. Key to that effort was the nurture of a steel and iron industry, centered initially on the government-run Yawata Steel Works based in Kyushu, and leading to the emergence of a steel juggernaut in the form of Japan Iron & Steel, Nippon Steel's antecedent, in 1934. After Japan's defeat in World War II in 1945, the powerful industrial conglomerates, *zaibatsu*, that had provided the material muscle for Imperial Japan, were ordered to disband by the Supreme Commander of the Allied Powers, General Douglas MacArthur. Japan Iron & Steel was dissolved and reformed as two new companies: Yawata Iron & Steel Co. and Fuji Iron & Steel Co. Twenty-five years later in 1970, the two companies "re-merged" to form Nippon Steel Corporation under calls to boost competitiveness under increasing global competition.

When in early 2006, Indian industrial tycoon Lakshmi Mittal made a successful takeover bid for Arcelor S.A., melding together the world's second-biggest steelmaker with the world's biggest, the mammoth ArcelorMittal S.A. company was formed. For its part, Nippon Steel was girding for a global battle with the right person at the helm in Akio Mimura, president from 2003 and chairman from 2008.

What Mimura brought to the table was a patented "old school" style of Japanese business that held persistence, diligence, and attention to detail as the highest virtues of business. Years of hard work from his school days had taught Mimura that there were no shortcuts to success outside hard work, patience, and a positive attitude. There was little reason to doubt that such attributes would yield results in any endeavor, which is why Mimura intentionally chose to join a company that was not leading its industry, but one that had strong ambitions to do so.

Mimura assumed leadership of Nippon Steel, and the steel industry as a whole, at a time when it needed a new mandate: a place in a postindustrialized world. The answer came in the form of creating the technological strength to produce the new highly functional steel and materials the future would require, and globalization, particularly as newly developing countries like China reinvigorated demand for steel. In this new global landscape, Nippon Steel did not possess the unquestionable driver of industry status it held for so long in Japan. It was second in the world, a position that seemed to have suited Mimura's personality perfectly. He helped lead Nippon Steel down a new path of expansion and reorganization aimed at making his company, and industry, viable and strong in a new century. By strengthening his alliance with Brazil's Usiminas, Mimura highlighted not only his ambitious nature to be number one, but confirmed his belief that attaining that high ground comes from hard work and persistence.

"All the blood, sweat, and tears shed by our predecessors at Nippon Steel in creating Usiminas are finally going to bear fruit after 50 years," remarked Mimura emotionally, upon making Nippon Usiminas a subsidiary.

As Mimura's successor, Shoji Muneoka, is committed to the same global aspirations for Nippon Steel centering on quality and technology to provide developed and emerging markets, such as BRIC nations, with the value-added, high-grade steel that will define and sustain Nippon Steel for years to come, while continuing to serve as a proud representative of Japanese industry by passing on the virtues of "patient management" and "constant innovation" to successive generations.

Principal Ideas of Akio Mimura and Shoji Muneoka

- Be exhaustive in debate, but quick in executing its conclusions.
- All companies suffer, but never indefinitely. Conversely, there's no guarantee that this year's good times will last into the next.
- Seek to balance demand with just the right capacity and a great sense of timing.

Nippon Steel Corp.

Established: April 1, 1970

Akio Mimura, Chairman

Shoji Muneoka, President and CEO

Head office: 2-6-1, Marunouchi, Chiyoda-ku, Tokyo

http://www.nsc.co.jp/

Capital: 419,500 million yen (year ending March 2009)

Consolidated sales: 4,769,821 million yen

Consolidated operating profit: 342,930 million yen

Consolidated net profit: 155,077 million yen

Employees: 50,077

10

ADVERSITY IS A REVERSAL OF FORTUNE OPPORTUNITY

Fumio Ohtsubo
President
Panasonic Corp.

Born September 5, 1945 in Osaka. Graduated from Kansai University's Graduate School of Science and Engineering and entered Matsushita Electric Co., Ltd. (Panasonic). Promoted to senior managing director in 2000, and president of Panasonic's AVC Network Company in 2002 focusing on audiovisual digital technologies. Named president of Matsushita Electric in 2006. Drew worldwide attention in January 2008 at the announcement of company name change to "Panasonic Corporation," and abolition of the "National" brand.

From Konosuke Matsushita to Fumio Ohtsubo

No substantial discussion on Japanese business over the past century could be adequately undertaken without the mention of Konosuke Matsushita. He was—and remains—a grand patriarch of modern industrial Japan. Although he passed away in April 1989, Matsushita continues to be passionately revered, his management philosophy eagerly studied and disseminated by Japanese young and old. An entire industry of books, seminars, and indeed even a major publishing company has grown up around the words, beliefs, and life of a man who began as an apprentice and in one generation built a colossal corporate entity called the Matsushita Electric Company. He is, like Henry Ford of the US, a man whose story defines an era, and whose legacy is immeasurable. In his waning years, Matsushita wanted to air the voice of the nation's youth and established the "Matsushita Institute of Government and Management" in hopes of cultivating the business and political leaders of the future, including many of the managers treated in the other chapters of this book.

There is a famous place in Japan that stands as a testament to Matsushita's achievements. It is the Kaminari *torii* gate and the giant lanterns that hang from its eaves at Kannon Shrine in Tokyo's oldest Asakusa district, and a requisite sight in every Tokyo guidebook. The gate and lantern at Asakusa Shrine actually stood half-built for nearly a century. Building costs had swollen so much that the project was left abandoned. Until 1960, Konosuke Matsushita donated money from his own pocket to restart construction. On the giant lantern, there is a plate with an inscription in gold letters: Konosuke Matsushita, Matsushita Electric Company. One of Japan's most frequented tourist sites is so today because of him.

Matsushita started what was called Matsushita Electric Devices Manufacturing Works out of a two-storey house in 1918. In 1935, it was rebadged Matsushita Electric, and would be so called for 90 years until 2008, when the company would make the landmark decision to consolidate all of its brands under the Panasonic moniker, thereby deleting the founder's name from the corporate title.

Under Matsushita Electric, three major brands evolved: Matsushita, National, and Panasonic, all existing alongside one another and each developing its own history, customer base, and brand equity. Merging these tradition-rich identities under one name must have stirred some emotions within the company. But the manager who ultimately made the decision, company president Fumio Ohtsubo, had made a passionate plea to "continue the process of destruction and creation."

The Panasonic name wasn't a first choice for Matsushita Electric half a century ago when the company sought to bring its National brand to the American market. The name was already owned by another company, so an alternative was chosen, Panasonic, and a multiple brand strategy became the norm for Matsushita.

For years, the name Matsushita was relatively little known outside of Japan. While Japanese companies such as Sony and Honda built globally recognized brands and products that bore the same name as the company, Matsushita Electric products were only recognized by overseas consumers through Panasonic, much like automaker Fuji Heavy Industries' Subaru automobile brand.

Mounting fears of an unprecedented global recession in late 2008 seemed to heighten the significance of large-scale reform initiatives that major Japanese companies had been undertaking or considering for quite some time. The decision to rename the company had been made by Ohtsubo, who had succeeded Kunio Nakamura, the Matsushita president largely credited for engineering the consumer electronics makers' V-shaped recovery during the economic morass of the 1990s in Japan. Ohtsubo and Nakamura believed the choice of a single, globally recognized name for the entire group would be an essential precondition to moving the company forward in an increasingly borderless world. But it was Ohtsubo who then dropped another bombshell when he announced Panasonic's intention to acquire struggling rival, Sanyo Electric, as a subsidiary.

Such moves, informed by years of restructuring that had already taken place, clearly reflected a keen awareness at Matsushita that to succeed in the current business climate and achieve sustained growth on a global scale would mean that no legacy or tradition, however entrenched or time honored, could take precedence over the need to stay current and relevant in a rapidly changing and volatile world.

"The name change signals a new start," Ohtsubo declared. "It is one way to rally our people and customers around a unified message and grow with a unified sense of purpose." Ohstubo suggested that the name change, though largely symbolic, would only begin to have real importance when every member of the company had embraced it personally.

Ohtsubo began his career at Panasonic in the recording device division where he quietly threw himself into improving product development and production techniques. His rise in the company would therefore be as a technician, and despite his shift to management, will always be driven most by a desire to raise technical expertise.

Ohtsubo's peers and bosses saw in him a responsible and committed worker who would patiently and diligently plug away at tasks until he could attain the desired results. In 1979, at 34 years of age, he was put in charge of 300 people as foreman of an equipment assembly line in the recording equipment division.

"A good education, a virtuous personality or a sharp mind are not necessary conditions for being a successful manager. Diligence, however, is. And practice. You need to apply yourself to each single task you're given, and appraise yourself honestly at every juncture. If you can do this day in and day out, you will acquire a knack for the business, and the ingredients for success."

Ohtsubo's thorough attention to factory floor issues earned him a post as president of a Matsushita audio manufacturing subsidiary in Singapore, eventually leading him to head up all of Matsushita's audio division, a slumping business that he succeeded in turning around.

Ohtsubo subscribes to an independent work and management style all his own, but one grounded in a decidedly heuristic approach. His predecessor, Kunio Nakamura, also operates from a highly independent mindset, which explains why these two have been the strongest agents of change the company has seen since its founder.

For better or for worse, the legacy of its founder has always loomed largest at Panasonic, and it has often been difficult to cultivate a climate of leadership independence as long as everyone continued to refer to it as "Mr. Matsushita's company."

When Kunio Nakamura became president, he brought with him a resolve to make everything that existed outside of the founder's core management philosophy a target for change. This was encapsulated in the idea of a "process of destruction and creation;" destroying that which seemed to cling to past successes, and creating that which stood for the achievement of greater value.

This new slogan led to a long-overdue process of consolidating and jettisoning brands at Matsushita to establish a more rational management architecture as a global company, but it also underscored a move away from a psychological dependence on the venerated founder. In this sense, the change in name from Matsushita Electric to Panasonic takes on added significance as the company looks to redefine itself in the eyes of the world.

Toward a V-shaped Recovery

After the bursting of the asset bubble in Japan in the early 1990s, then Panasonic president Akio Tanii tried valiantly to overhaul his hard-hit company, only to be roiled again by the collapse of the dotcom bubble in the US a few years later. Nothing has come easily since.

But the effect that these crises had—the former being relegated primarily to Japan—was to set in motion the types of reforms that would eventually be necessary in the twenty-first century, and in the face of subsequent crises including the global recession of 2008–09. The changes had to be epochal in nature, and they were.

They began with the complete dismantling of a tradition-ensconced, corporate division-based system that Konosuke Matsushita himself had cherished, and taking a chisel to an organization that had grown too wieldy and calcified. The large-scale reforms included accepting the voluntary retirement of 13,000 workers, abolishing or merging unprofitable divisions, converting some primary affiliates into full subsidiaries, and redrawing the company's business lines.

Reducing costs proved the most painful, though unavoidable. Inviolable Japanese businesses practices that had served the country well during its miracle growth years—lifetime employment, seniority-based promotions—were now being viewed as unsustainable in the low-growth economy of the future. As unemployment offices swelled with unemployed white-collar workers, once the pillars of society but now a "restructured" diaspora with few specialized skills, voices rose in warning against the catastrophic effects of a collapse of the nation's social safety net.

While the long-term effects of this period are yet to be fully grasped, Japanese companies like Panasonic knew that amid the retrenchment, there could be no compromising on manufacturing quality and product development. In a country with little natural resources, innovation would be the only path to recovery. Panasonic, for example, seeing new opportunities in the emerging IT age, launched a new product assault in the consumer appliance space with digital products such as the Viera plasma television and Diga DVD recorders. Coupled with ongoing internal reform efforts, product development around emergent technologies and markets brought about the V-shaped recovery Nakamura sought.

Unfortunately, boom cycles seem to have grown shorter and shorter. The digital appliance revolution that saved Panasonic from near collapse began to fizzle out amid slumping consumer demand, and Panasonic slipped back into the red just as a global recession loomed.

With Fumio Ohtsubo at the helm, structural reforms were again underway. Poorly performing divisions and facilities were put on the chopping block and the workforce was reduced. But this time, it was done more quickly, with cuts not sinking quite as deeply. As a result, though it is still too early to tell at the writing of this book, earlier drastic reform efforts and the directions being taken by the new Panasonic currently have prompted many industry observers to predict that among Japanese consumer electronics makers, Panasonic is the one that should recover the fastest once the global downturn recedes. In the words of Konosuke Matsushita himself:

> There are no times of boom or bust for the merchant. Whatever the circumstances, you must generate wealth.

Destroying Old Tradition, Creating New Value

Fumio Ohtsubo earned a master's degree in engineering from Kansai University, and became the consummate shopfloor technician in his early days at Panasonic's audio division. In Ohtsubo, current Panasonic chairman, Kunio Nakamura, saw what he believed to be the perfect embodiment of the other half of his philosophy, "creation." Nakamura had represented the "destruction" part of the equation. He had with great sense of purpose and personal energy moved the company out from under the immense shadow of founder Konosuke Matsushita, exposing it to new light and tearing down some of its musty rafters. All that was needed now to complete the transformation from Matsushita Electric to Panasonic would be for Nakamura the "destructionist" to work well with Ohtsubo the "creationist" and let that *yin–yang* dynamic guide an ongoing strategy of "selection and focus."

Both men believed it essential to rationalize further and streamline their organization to make it more market sensitive and responsive. This lay at the heart of the founder's philosophy of making something essential for the people of the nation. When Konosuke Matsushita developed a portable battery-operated lamp that could be used as a handheld flashlight or a bicycle light, he named it the "national lamp," because it would hopefully serve the needs of a nation. From that product, the "National" brand was born. Nakamura and Ohtsubo seek to build, in figurative terms, a "global lamp."

Aggressive Development of Next-Generation Technologies

"We need to shift to a new age where we each and every employee can consider himself the main protagonist in our company's activities, and do away with relying solely on the greatness and charisma of our founder. That is how we will develop with a great sense of purpose and energy the next great technologies of the future."

Ohtsubo drew a specific example:

I'm talking about battery technology, in particular, rechargeable NiMH, lithium-ion, and solar batteries. Our pending acquisition of Sanyo Electric as a full subsidiary has been motivated in large part by its strength in this area. If we see mutual synergies can be reaped through mergers and acquisitions, then those are the directions we need to pursue.

For the past several years, Sanyo Electric, too, has struggled. Sales of its white goods (refrigerators, washers, and other home appliances) have dropped and the company as a whole barely broke even in fiscal 2008. But one area where Sanyo has seen success is in its new "eneloop" brand of rechargeable Ni-MH batteries and other eneloop consumer products. The simple elegant design of the products is meant to evoke an eco-friendly, new age style of life, and include solar batteries, air purifiers, and energy-efficient lights. It is a field that both Sanyo and Panasonic view as having enormous growth potential given a growing environmental and energy-efficient consciousness among consumers, with a boom in portable music players and other digital devices.

As illustrated in Konosuke's bicycle-light invention, Panasonic has traditionally been strong in battery technology and, together with Sanyo, will dominate the home-use, rechargeable battery segment. While there is some overlap, the expected gains are great if they can efficiently merge the operations. Panasonic and Sanyo have projected that, together, they can boost operating revenue by 80 billion yen by 2012.

"Because the current economic instability has clouded the immediate future, bold moves that can spark change are needed," Ohtsubo contends. "By pooling our technological assets and manufacturing strengths, we think we can increase our ability to compete and maximize corporate value."

Ohtsubo is also bullish about the synergies the acquisition of Sanyo will produce in the highly promising field of automotive batteries and electronics.

"We have set a sales target of one trillion yen in the area of car electronics, and Sanyo will most surely be the growth engine there. Global attention is once again turning to the hybrid car, which is proving a bright spot in these recessionary times, and we foresee a great increase in demand for second-generation batteries used in electric vehicles when they become mainstream. Both of us work with different automakers for joint technology development, but we are certain that our partnership will yield enormous benefits to every automaker."

Indeed, Sanyo provides batteries for both the Toyota Prius and the Honda Insight, both gas-electric hybrid cars, and sales of the Toyota Prius have been skyrocketing amid the global downturn. Sanyo also possesses leading technology for converting gas-electric hybrids to plug-in hybrid vehicles slated to be market ready by 2011. Plug-in hybrids would allow owners to recharge their vehicles (lithium-ion rechargeable battery) at home using standard electrical outlets. Current gas-electric hybrids recharge the electric battery through the vehicle's motion, but plug-in hybrids would house a higher capacity battery and allow the vehicle to run three times longer (about 60 km) than a gas-electric hybrid on simply the electric motor. The biggest hurdle remains the need to reduce battery size while sustaining that performance. But there's no denying that automakers are increasingly relying on employing the advanced battery technologies of electric makers like Sanyo. Ultimately, the union with Sanyo gives Panasonic a great jump on its competition toward top share in the lucrative automotive energy sector of the future.

Big changes are also taking place inside the Panasonic Group of companies. Panasonic Electric Works Co., which had primarily made lighting fixtures and electrical equipment, announced on September 17, 2009 that it would start making and selling electric vehicle recharging stands, dubbed ELSEEV, for 200-volt sockets set up outdoors. While conventional estimates put the cost per "pump" at about four million yen, Panasonic says it has managed to lower that cost to about 200,000 yen, or one-twentieth. The tradeoff for the low price is that the stands would recharge vehicles at slow, standard household socket speeds, but Panasonic hopes to sell 10,000 of these standalone rechargers in 2011 to public facilities such as libraries, or for use in company parking lots. ELSEEV may be one of the more immediate results of Panasonic's expansion into the energy business with Sanyo.

Along with secondary batteries, Sanyo also possesses world-class technology and know-how in solar cells. If Sanyo maximizes its strength in product development in the field of electronic components, commercial cooling equipment, and digital imaging such as digital cameras, then total energy management solutions for homes and commercial buildings could constitute a sizable percentage of Panasonic's future earnings.

In short, the union with Sanyo gives Panasonic good reason to expect a boost to all its energy related businesses. Panasonic is building a dedicated lithium-ion battery plant in Osaka with production slated to begin in October 2009 and plans to spend 123 billion yen over the next five years in capital investment.

For its part, Sanyo is looking to ramp up production of lithium-ion batteries in massive quantities starting 2009 for use primarily in gas-electric hybrid vehicles, and plans to invest some 80 billion yen over the next six years in the segment.

Panasonic also benefits from immediate growth by acquiring Sanyo, raising total earnings to 11 trillion yen, and surpassing Hitachi as Japan's largest electronics maker. The extent to which Ohtsubo can recast Panasonic as a global leader in the energy products and services field will likely hinge on the success of merging Sanyo's units with his own. But one thing is certain. Under Ohtsubo, Panasonic has certainly embarked upon the "creation" side of Nakamura's equation.

Energy is not the only area that Panasonic is banking on for new growth. In additional to traditional audio-visual products and white goods, Ohtsubo is anxious to develop new products for its "volume zone," namely, capturing demand among middle-income customers in BRICs and other emerging economies. Despite the conventional wisdom that value-added, state-of-the-art products are hard to sell in emerging countries, it would be hard to resist catering to the immense purchasing power that is likely to be released in these high-volume markets once the global economy recovers from the recession of 2008.

In other words, Panasonic can be expected to follow a two-pronged global strategy that seeks to boost its offering of products and services in the field of energy in advanced countries, and bringing its audio visual and white goods products along with services deeply rooted in local communities to newly industrializing parts of the world.

Among the hundreds of famous shards of wisdom uttered by Panasonic founder, Konosuke Matsushita, there is one in particular, uttered to his charges at the launch of a new product, that speaks strongly to the "destroy and create" culture on which Fumio Ohtsubo and his predecessor, Akio Nakamura, have sought to revive their company.

"Good work. You have made something truly great here. Now go and get started on a new product that will make this one obsolete."

If one were to try to extrapolate the serious directives of this light-hearted quip, one might interpret them as: always possessing an inexhaustible inquisitiveness, always keeping one's eyes set on new goals ahead toward which to strive, and continually seeking to outdo yourself in your next endeavor. Because therein lies the secret to success.

Summary: Outgrowing One Legacy to Create a New One

The Matsushita Electric Devices Manufacturing Works founded by Konosuke Matsushita in 1918 underwent its first name change in 1935 to Matsushita Electric Industrial Company. Seventy-five years later, the name would be changed again in October 2008 to "Panasonic," bringing its three parallel brands of "Matsushita," "National," and "Panasonic" under one moniker to represent both the company and the brand.

Panasonic President Fumio Ohtsubo, still relatively new in his leadership role after just over two years, justified the move as part and parcel of an ongoing companywide philosophy dubbed "destruction and creation." This philosophy would be immediately tested shortly after with the announced bankruptcy of 160-year-old financial services giant Lehman Brothers sparking a meltdown in financial markets and a global recession. Yet as companies around the world tightened their spigots on capital and capital spending, Ohtsubo decided to acquire Sanyo Electric Co. in a bid to become Japan's largest electronics maker, and seek sustained growth in promising sectors such as next-generation batteries for gas-electric hybrid motors and opening newly industrializing markets like China.

For better or for worse, Panasonic had always been a company built and sustained by the legacy of its charismatic leader, Konosuke Matsushita. It was therefore hard to cultivate a climate of independent leadership among managers. They were more like stewards of "Mr. Matsushita's company." Panasonic could draw strength from the hallowed *monozukuri* (manufacturing) spirit and management philosophy of its esteemed founder. But as a strong believer in empowerment, Chairman Kunio Nakamura encouraged a change in mindset at Panasonic to focus on the individual, not the charismatic founder, as the central player in the company: a stance he believed necessary for establishing the customer-first viewpoint that the times demand.

In the decade of stagnant economic growth that followed the collapse of the asset-price bubble in Japan in the early 1990s, Kunio Nakamura came to the fore to revive his company under the mantra of "destruction and creation," vowing to change everything but the founder's core business philosophy. He would seek to destroy legacy clingings to past successes in favor of creating a new company that could perpetually rise to market demands.

But Nakamura's rise to the Panasonic presidency in June 2000 was accompanied by unfortunate timing; the height of the dotcom crash. Instead of a new beginning, Nakamura had to bear the stain of being at the helm when Matsushita posted the first deficit in its 80-year history for 2001. "Creation" would have to be put on hold. Instead, Nakamura had to undertake a massive restructuring plan. He called for 13,000 voluntary retirees, primarily middle managers, spun off or abolished nonperforming units, eliminated the company's time-honored but wieldy division system established by the founder himself; and brought sister affiliate companies under one roof as subsidiaries. Running tandem with these austerity measures, he also planted the seeds for a V-shaped recovery by launching a new product assault in digital consumer electronics such as the plasma television, Viera, and the DVD recorder, Diga. In the July 12 edition of *BusinessWeek*, Nakamura was selected as one of "Asia's top 25 business leaders." The magazine introduced his effort as a case study in restructuring an ineffectively large legacy company through reorganization and development of strong new products. Once the series of reforms had yielded a certain level of recovery, Nakamura unhesitatingly relinquished the presidency to Fumio Ohtsubo, a man with an engineering background, and became chairman.

In contrast to Nakamura, who had studied Japanese economics and history as an economics major at Osaka University, and had moved around Osaka University, and had moved around a lot at Panasonic, at one point serving in a US branch, Fumio Ohtsubo graduated from the graduate school of science and engineering at Kansai University (also in Osaka) and built up his corporate experience in the manufacturing floors of the audio division. To Nakamura, who had invested so much energy in the "dismantling" part of his revival strategy, Ohtsubo seemed someone he could entrust with the "creation" part as well as continue the key "selection and focus" strategy of the Nakamura reforms. Ohtsubo himself came into the job believing that "growth" was his mission.

When a global recession hit in the fall of 2008 after "the Lehman Shock," sales for digital appliances plummeted sending Panasonic back into the red for the year ending March 2009.

In an uncanny refrain to Nakamura's tenure as president, the man slated for "creation" now finds himself forced to do some dismantling of his own. But along with carrying out workforce reductions and closing poorly performing divisions and bases, Ohtsubo has begun mapping out a series of new long-term reforms aimed at getting the company ready to hit the ground running when markets recover. This includes acquiring Sanyo Electric as a subsidiary with its strengths in promising fields of next-generation lithium-ion batteries and solar cells, as well as a shift to lower-priced digital home appliances for markets like China and India.

Ohtsubo comes armed with the strong branding, powerful R&D and cutting-edge digital technologies necessary to turn Panasonic into a top, consumer-driven and agile global company capable of responding adeptly to structural changes in the market, from the rise of BRIC nations to a global recession. Yet even amid all this change, Ohtsubo still looks to the management philosophy of the company's venerated founder, Konosuke Matsushita.

"We will continue to adhere in all our business activities to the core ideals of this management philosophy," Ohtsubo writes on Panasonic's global website; defining a company as a public entity that understands the primacy of the "customer-comes-first" principle, the need to "start fresh every day," and to practice "management by all with collective wisdom."

Principal Ideas of Fumio Ohtsubo

- Shift to a mindset that views each employee as protagonist.
- Act as an agent of change particularly in times of economic and future instability.
- Be inquisitive, set goals toward which to strive and continually try to outdo yourself.

Panasonic Corp.

Established: December 15, 1935
Fumio Ohtsubo, President
Head office: 1006, Kadoma, Kadoma City, Osaka
http://www.panasonic.net/
Capital: 258,740 million yen (year ending March 2009)
Consolidated sales: 7,765,507 million yen
Consolidated operating profit: 72,873 million yen
Consolidated net profit: −378,961 million yen
Employees: 292,250

11

WHEN BUSINESS MUST NOT COME FIRST

Yasuchika Hasegawa
President
Takeda Pharmaceutical Co., Ltd.

Born June 1946, Yamaguchi Prefecture. Graduated from Waseda University's School of Political Science and Economics and Joined Takeda Pharmaceutical Company. Served as president of TAP Pharmaceutical Products (a joint venture between US Abbot Laboratories and Takeda Pharmaceutical Co.), and spent 10 years in the US general manager of the Pharmaceutical International Division. Elected member of the board in 1999, and then general manager of the Corporate Planning Dept. and general manager of the Corporate Strategy and Planning Dept., before being appointed Takeda president in 2003. Also serves as vice chairman of Keizai Doyukai (Japan Association of Corporate Executives).

From Middleman (Broker) to Medicine Maker

Takeda Pharmaceutical is the largest pharmaceutical company in Japan, and has been a very visible and trusted brand in the country for more than two centuries. But as with every large and long-surviving Japanese company, it faces limitations of growth in a shrinking domestic market and the steep challenges of remaining competitive in an increasingly global and capital-intensive industry. In short, Takeda needs to make the leap to major global player status.

Strive "toward better health for individuals and progress in medicine by developing superior pharmaceutical products on a global scale" is the company's mission, as stated by president Yasuchika Hasegawa. "Takeda-ism" is the corporate philosophy that sets the tone for all of Takeda's activities. It is defined on the corporate website as: "Contributing to society through (a) determination to continue expanding the business of creating medicines through corporate activities based on integrity (fairness, honesty and perseverance)." Hasegawa goes on to say that Takeda-ism has "continuously guided the company throughout its more than 220 years . . ." and that any "future business undertakings will never deviate from these core values."

The core values espoused by Takeda-ism, then, predate the US Constitutional Convention; they predate the French Revolution. For Takeda was founded in 1781, at the height of the Edo Period (1603–1868). Takeda's founder was a 32-year-old Osaka native named Chobei Takeda, who opened a small business divvying up medicinal products from wholesalers into small batches and selling them around town. He was a traveling pharmacist, the last rung in a supply chain. But from such humble peripatetic beginnings, Takeda Pharmaceutical was born.

Chobei Takeda hailed from a town in Japan's ancient capital of Nara some 19 miles away from where he plied his trade, which he entered as an apprentice to another medicine broker by the name of Kisuke Ohmiya. When Takeda was ready to strike out on his own, his mentor bequeathed half of the business to his pupil.

As tradition would have it in these times, every succeeding owner of the business had to take on the name Chobei, and pass that name on to his successor. So Chobei Takeda II followed Chobei Takeda 1, and so forth. It was Chobei Takeda IV who decided to add a little twist to the family trade by buying small quantities of imported Western medicines. The 18 varieties of "Western medicine" that were entering Japan at the time included quinine for treating malaria and carbolic acid to fight cholera.

By 1895, demand for medicines of all kinds had grown enough for Chobei IV to expand from being a medicine purveyor to manufacturing. He used his savings to build a factory in Osaka producing quinine hydrochloride and anti-diarrheal agents, and marking the true beginnings of Takeda as a pharma company.

In 1925, under Chobei Takeda V, the family business was at last incorporated as a pharmaceutical company under the name Chobei Takeda & Co., Ltd. Until then, it had been operated as an individually owned business, but now took on the form and functions of a modern corporate organization. The company would then change its name in 1943 to Takeda Chemical Industries, Ltd.

From there, Takeda grew through production and sales of medicinal products. But the first major breakthrough came in 1954 with the launch of a vitamin B1 derivative sold under the name Alinamine. It brought company national fame.

Among pharmaceutical companies of the time, Takeda proved to be particularly aggressive in its product development, and the company worked hard to expand its lineup of drugs that were easily accessible to the average citizen. By doing so, Takeda earned widespread consumer support until it had grown into the nation's largest and most recognized pharmaceutical company.

It is to the great credit of a strong management foundation, and "Takeda-ism," that even after 200 years, some of the greatest achievements at Takeda were still to come. In the 1990s, when Kunio Takeda, a scion of the founding family, became company president, Japan was reeling from a post-bubble economic malaise and trying to come to terms with a new paradigm of low-to-no growth. In spite of this, Kunio Takeda managed to achieve high profit margins by undertaking bold personnel reforms and applying a "selection and focus" approach, much like Akio Nakamura did at Panasonic. By the time he was finished reforming, he'd built Takeda into a trillion-yen company.

Like Panasonic, a new manager, viewed as embodying the company's core values yet also capable of articulating a new mandate for the company in the twenty-first century, was tapped to be president. Yasuchika Hasegawa came to the job with 13 years of overseas working experience, and was seen as the perfect man to lead a global charge aimed at doubling Takeda's earnings to the two trillion-yen plateau.

The New "Takeda-ism"

For 12 consecutive years, Takeda Pharmaceutical has set new highs in earnings. "There's no magic to running a business," Hasegawa is fond of saying. Though a true-blooded disciple of "Takeda-ism," Hasegawa, from the moment he took office in 2003, has dared to walk a different path from his predecessor, Kunio Takeda, who was considered one of Takeda's most charismatic leaders to date. Before Hasegawa's appointment, the company had prided itself on a strong and successful culture of self-reliance in new drug development. But Hasegawa immediately questioned that assumption.

Hasegawa believes that no company can ever expect to have a monopoly on good ideas, and pharma companies are finding it increasingly harder and more costly to count on exclusive in-house development of the next breakthrough drug. You need actively to go out and look for the kinds of materials that lead to breakthrough drugs. Hasegawa is therefore not shy about wanting to make key strategic acquisitions.

Kunio Takeda, who grew the company into a trillion-yen enterprise, agrees:

> In the past 10 years or so, we actively did away with some of our traditional businesses such as our food products division to better concentrate our energy and resources on our core competency: developing and manufacturing drugs. I think that has allowed us to build the financial strength to go global. But then the question becomes how best to spend our cash. Well, with our new organization, I think we can use that money effectively and wisely through acquisitions in addition to our own research, and that gives us great hope for the future.

Expectations are high for Hasegawa as the right man to spearhead the global drive and make all the right moves. His professional background and track record indicate that he can. But his was a career that could have just as easily never materialized:

> When I first entered the company, I was placed in the G&A section in a factory. It was work I had a hard time adapting to, and very little went as I expected. I made a lot of mistakes. I didn't find out until much later that it was a section that new employees almost never got assigned to. In other words, no one had ever stuck around for very long after being placed there. I don't know what got me posted there in the first place, whether it was for character building or to get rid of me. But it's where I was able to make—and learn from—a lot of mistakes.

Even if one isn't new to the job, the G&A section was tasked with mediating and resolving any personnel troubles. So resolving sticky situations was the job. But Hasegawa persisted, enduring many tribulations and challenges as he carried out his duties:

I still feel much the same as I did back then. The reason I didn't just quit right away was probably because even if things went terribly wrong, I never felt compelled to cover up those failings or lie about them. Failures are what you want to avoid, of course, but if and when they do occur—and they will—it is important to limit the damage as much as you can. You can't turn back the clock but you can learn from your mistakes.

Hasegawa often speaks of the importance of damage control through quick response, after which he advocates taking a sure, steady, and honest approach to building results and ensuring that mistakes aren't repeated.

Hasegawa says he learned to tame what was an impatient streak in his personality and "lend an ear to the voices around him, to be deliberate, fair, and thorough in discussions, but then prompt in action."

As a result, face-to-face exchanges of views with many people, though often time consuming, is an important facet of Hasegawa's leadership style. It has earned him high approval among employees. Employees on the factory floors or in the field know that their views, at the very least, will get the president's ear, and at most, can influence or shape company policy. From the management standpoint, listening to as many people as possible not only invariably leads to better choices, but also is the surest means for managing risk.

Since there is no proven method for best ensuring all voices are heard, Hasegawa contends that face-to-face interactions remain the best means when they are possible, but that other forms of communication, be it email or fax, can do the job. The important thing is ensuring that two-way communication is taking place.

From childhood, Hasegawa was never ordered by his parents to study. Instead, they encouraged him to go outside and play to his heart's content, something relatively unheard of in Japan where extracurricular cram schools are ubiquitous and start at grade school level. Upon returning home from school, Hasegawa would immediately race back out the door to play in the hills behind his home. He wouldn't come back until nightfall. Hasegawa took to learning by watching and imitating, and once even caught a bird in a makeshift trap he'd set. At that age, just running up and down a mountain road provided ample fun and stimulation, but what he really loved was sumo wrestling with his friends. If he lost, he'd continue at it until he won. This never-say-die attitude would serve him well at Takeda from those early days in the G&A section to today.

Be Prepared for When Opportunity Comes Knocking

Takeda has cruised along as the number one pharma company in Japan, but has hovered over the past 10-plus years between fifteenth and twentieth globally. Takeda's in-house ethical drugs remain its core business, accounting for about 90 percent of total net sales and providing the earnings for further development and acquisitions. These drugs for treating such "lifestyle-related diseases" as diabetes, hypertension, and gastrointestinal diseases such as peptic ulcers are marketed in 90 countries around the world, and are an ongoing key to Takeda's global strategy.

While Takeda boasted annual sales of 1.5 trillion yen at the end of 2008, it still lags far behind in competing with Pfizer and GlaxoSmithKline, both of which double Takeda in size. Takeda's 2008 purchase of American biopharmaceutical company, Millennium Pharmaceuticals of Boston, for close to 900 billion yen showed that Takeda is serious about growing globally.

Pharmaceutical companies at present are engaged in some of the fiercest competition ever seen as a result of deregulation of drugs. The world's top 20 so-called "Big Pharma" companies, while owning nearly 60 percent of the global market, are fighting over razor-thin differences in share with no one company in double digits. None of these companies can afford to rely solely only on their domestic markets for growth, particularly when R&D costs to bring a single drug to market exceeds a billion dollars per drug.

Rival foreign companies have grown into enormous entities owing to aggressive consolidation and realignment. Takeda has been ramping up overseas operations as much as possible over the past few years, acquiring biotech startups. While the global economic downturn may dampen that progress, Hasegawa says that it's all about staying the course:

> It's a matter of executing properly and doing what we have to do with a surefootedness about us as we look toward the future landscape of global pharma companies. No matter what process unfolds, the bottom line is whether you can produce new revolutionary and beneficial drugs. At least for as long

as I am the president of this company, I must produce those kinds of results. I try to motivate myself to raise the bar as high as I can every day. I try to confront things I would rather not think about in hopes of making some daily progress on them. In other words, it's important to never be satisfied with the status quo.

High Quality Begets Trust

At the announcement of the company's results for fiscal 2008, Hasegawa surprised those in attendance with a harsh indictment of the company's R&D mentality. "I feel we've often placed too much emphasis on speed and volume, and that doesn't always lead to favorable results." Then Hasegawa offered up a new direction:

> Let's shift our R&D focus so that it prioritizes quality above all else, and bring to the market very unique products that consistently fulfill unmet needs.

In April 2008, Takeda spent nearly nine billion dollars to acquire one of the first genomic companies in the US, the Cambridge Massachusetts-based Millennium Pharmaceutical. The aim is to strengthen Takeda's cancer research.

Said Hasegawa: "The benefits we get from Millennium as a company located in the bioscience-cluster around Boston are immeasurable. The Millennium acquisition is great not just because it has a strong record in working with the FDA, but because it does cutting-edge research in cancer as well as immune science and biotechnology-based medicine."

Millennium was the largest deal ever for a Japanese drugmaker. It must have been quite significant on the US side as well. Hasegawa threw out the first pitch at a Boston Red Sox baseball game in May of 2009:

> We need to set up new controller positions for R&D, overseas sales networks, and management supervision to give greater responsibility to *genba*, the shopfloor. The urgent aim is to speed up management as we go increasingly global.

Already, Takeda has expanded sales networks in Canada, Spain, Portugal, and Ireland, along with the construction of a global management system centered on regional bases in London, Singapore, and Chicago. But Takeda still relies on the US market for 40 percent of its earnings.

"We've been negatively affected by the economic downturn in the US long before the Obama administration announced its plans to overhaul the healthcare system," notes Hasegawa. With growth expected to be stunted in the US pharmaceutical market for the immediate future, Hasegawa is eager to cultivate new channels in places such as Canada, Spain, and the UK.

One of Takeda's distinctive traits is the high margins it earns. In 2006, the company posted an operating income margin of 35 percent!

"This is very high even in a high-margin industry like pharmaceuticals," Hasegawa noted. "I believe that among the world's top 20 firms, only Takeda and Amgen of the US have hit those margin levels at this point."

Hasegawa sees these results as a manifestation of "Takeda-ism":

A manager needs to be fearless at times. I don't just mean having the courage to start something wholly new, but more importantly the willingness to pull the plug. This is actually quite important because it is still relatively foreign to Japanese business. Japanese managers haven't been very good at this in the past. In principle, everyone understands that although a person may have spent years contributing to a company, if at some point that person can no longer produce results for the company, then a change must be made. That may be the toughest job a manager has to face. But if you fail to do what is necessary, you're not only doing a disservice to that person, you're weakening the entire organization. Strengthening the organization is the job of the company manager.

Hasegawa expects a lot from his people, believing a company is only as strong as its weakest link. He is what most would call "a true believer," with high ideals. To achieve the goals he raises, each employee is expected to possess ambitions as lofty as his:

A few years ago, we had a consumer management department that suffered from a high attrition rate. When I told everyone in the department to quickly address this problem, one member told me that this was simply a common condition in companies everywhere right now. I wasn't expecting that. Feeling very vexed and disappointed, I called that employee in and basically gave him a piece of my mind. "The notion that the problem is everywhere doesn't make it okay," I told him. In his mind, then, we were no different than any other company.

If there are parts of your organization that have clearly gone astray, you mustn't waste time. You must move right away to improve things. Don't expect problems to work themselves out over time. That goes for leadership, too. You must be able to detect and respond to challenges early. Having an indomitable will and never giving up is what Takeda-ism is all about.

As with Fast Retailing's Tadashi Yanai, Yasuchika Hasegawa's management style is based on open and honest engagement with his employees, which can involve just as much scolding as it does praise. "There is a cultural tendency in Japan not to say exactly what you mean," laments Hasegawa, who has little patience for mind games. This must change as companies expand globally and take on a more international work force. If Hasegawa can cast the virtues of a two-century-old business philosophy—patience and perseverance—into a contemporary and global mold that values speed, openness, and diversity, then perhaps he will show the world how a company can endure and grow indefinitely.

Summary: Toward the Next 200 Years

With a history that dates back to 1781, Takeda Pharmaceutical is one of Japan's oldest surviving companies. It began with a man peddling Japanese medicine in Osaka and building a family business. In those days, businesses and customer trust were largely built on family name. So one needed to retain that name, either through bloodline or adopting an apprentice. This is how it remained at Takeda for nearly two centuries. In 1974, Chobei Takeda became the company's sixth president. But his third son, Kunio Takeda, who rose to the presidency in 1993 took an axe to convention, and struck out on an aggressive growth strategy aimed at turning the tradition-bound family business into a global entity. With Kunio, the dynastic succession would end.

Kunio's older brother was the one originally primed to become the seventh Chobei Takeda, but passed away right before taking office. When Kunio became president, he chose not to take on the name "Chobei," but instead instituted some major reforms such as adopting an outward-looking business stance, and doing away with nonpharmaceutical divisions to better concentrate on medicine. Kunio also shook up traditional management practices, such as introducing performance-based promotions. All this was done with a sense of urgency and crisis, as Kunio believed 200 years of tradition could in many respects do more harm than good in keeping the company current. Kunio then went and hand-picked a successor in Yasuchika Hasegawa who was not from the Takeda clan, and stepped away from day-to-day management. He became chairman but in 2009 retired from the board of directors. Meanwhile Hasegawa, born in 1946, was a postwar child who could use his rich international experience to reshape Japan's biggest pharmaceutical company into one of the world's top 10.

Kunio Takeda often draws comparisons to Canon's Fujio Mitarai and Toyota's Shoichiro Toyoda as a direct descendant of an oligarchical business family who chose reform over preserving a dynastic bloodline. Each felt it his mission as a manager to promote rationalism over tradition and talent over lineage as a necessary means for ensuring company survival in the ruggedly competitive world of the twenty-first century.

Japan is home to a large number of centenarian companies. Many of them have survived through a keen understanding of a traditional mercantile philosophy in Japan that advocates always taking a measured approach to temporal trends, and carefully weighing benefits against risks instead of looking for the quick and easy profit. The best of these have not hesitated to promote talent over lineage to ensure the rational leadership necessary to keep the company relevant and vital over the long haul.

Kunio Takeda first noticed Hasegawa's potential in the late 1980s when Hasegawa was vice-president of TAP Pharmaceutical Products (a joint venture between US Abbott Laboratories and Takeda Pharmaceutical Co.) in Chicago. Kunio himself had served in the same role previously, and had been a part of Takeda's first major success in the US with the advanced prostate cancer treatment drug, Lupron. The success of that product funded further research and development (R&D) of major drugs. Hasegawa, too, as president at TAP oversaw the development of a highly successful ulcer treatment drug called Prevacid.

TAP became a full subsidiary of Takeda in 2008, and together with the purchase of Millennium that same year, will play an increasingly important role in Takeda's global growth strategy, particularly in filling the pipeline with promising new drugs just as the exclusive patents on many of Takeda's flagship drugs expire.

"Good luck comes only after one has sufficiently created the conditions for it," Hasegawa is fond of saying, paraphrasing from the Alex Rovira book, *Good Luck: Creating the Conditions for Success in Business and Life.*

While Kunio Takeda had the top-down leadership charisma and bloodline credibility to bring about tremendous reform of a legacy company, Hasegawa believes more in a bottom-up approach and team play. In a talk he gave in Tokyo as vice chairman of the Japan Association of Corporate Executives in July 2008, Hasegawa laid out what he believed were the strengths and weaknesses of Japanese-style management, and what changes needed to be made to boost competitiveness in lieu of the current business environment. Teamwork, loyalty, a strong emphasis on quality and safety, a long-term view, consensus-based precision implementation, integrated information exchange, and an ability to improve production processes, technologies, and products continuously were the strengths. The areas he saw as in need of change were more national and ethnic diversity in organizations, better foreign language proficiency, and more of an emphasis on contractual rather than ambiguous "trust" relationships. These he views as managerial weaknesses, or differences between the West and East, that will have to be skillfully reconciled if the Takeda Pharmaceutical Company is to become a truly top global company for the next two-plus centuries.

Principal Ideas of Yasuchika Hasegawa

- Good luck comes only after one has sufficiently created the conditions for it.

- Lend an ample ear to the voices around you, but then be prompt and decisive in action.

- Never be satisfied with the status quo, but try to raise the bar as high as possible each day.

Takeda Pharmaceutical Co., Ltd.

Established: June 1782
Yasuchika Hasegawa, President and CEO
Head office: 4-1-1, Doshomachi, Chuo-ku, Osaka City
http://www.takeda.com/
Capital: 63,541 million yen (year ending March 2009)
Consolidated sales: 1,538,336 million yen
Consolidated operating profit: 306,468 million yen
Consolidated net profit: 234,385 million yen
Employees: 19,362

12

WINNING IN THE NEW WORKPLACE

Masahiro Sakane
Chairman
Komatsu Ltd.

Born January 1941. Shimane Prefecture. Graduated from Osaka City University, Faculty of Engineering in 1963, and joined Komatsu. Appointed president of Komatsu Dresser Company in 1990 (currently, Komatsu America Corp.). Served as president and CEO of Komatsu Ltd. from June 2001. Became chairman in 2007.

World War II Revealed Yawning Technology Gap

It was 1941, immediately after the December 7 attack on Pearl Harbor. The Japanese military machine fanned out through Asia, occupying formerly American-held positions in the region. But what the Japanese army saw as they marched in to occupy posts left by fleeing American and allied forces was construction machinery, lots of it, namely, bulldozers. They couldn't believe their eyes. Japan itself had been engaged in construction equipment research at its top universities before the war, but they were far from producing much that was field ready, and nothing seemed to work to their satisfaction.

In contrast to the small hand-operated farm equipment that had been used to tame the land in Japan, the American bulldozers were a marvel of technology. In the blink of an eye, whole tracts of rugged wilderness could be leveled into well-groomed pastureland. Work that normally required dozens of men several weeks to complete could be handled by one bulldozer in a matter of hours.

For many Japanese, particularly soldiers in the Japanese Imperial Army and Navy, the sight of all those bulldozers was at once captivating and disheartening. Soldiers were said to be heard murmuring that against such technological might, there was no way Japan could win the war.

Before the war, Meitaro Takeuchi, founder of Komatsu Ltd., had already been thoroughly impressed at seeing American bulldozers at work, so much so that it inspired him to begin trying to build construction machinery himself. When Komatsu came into possession of one of the bulldozers left behind by the US, the military government of Japan ordered it to be reverse engineered with the hope that a domestically produced bulldozer might make it into the field in time to aid the war effort.

Up until that point, Komatsu was an in-house unit of Takeuchi Mining Industry, of which Meitaro Takeuchi was president, manufacturing machine tools and mining equipment. When Komatsu Iron Works became an independent company in 1921 as Komatsu Ltd., the timing could not have been worse. It faced several crises within its first couple of years, two of them devastating: the 1923 Great Kanto Earthquake and the 1927 Showa Financial Crisis.

Komatsu struggled to survive until the 1930s. But it was the Mukden Incident in China in 1931 leading to the Japanese occupation of Manchuria that opened up new markets for Komatsu products in both Manchuria and on the Korean peninsula. Komatsu began to build farm tractors, Japan's first, and did manage to produce primitive military-use bulldozers for the war, along with tractors and tanks. But it wasn't until two years after the end of World War II that Komatsu succeeded in producing a serviceable commercial bulldozer called the G40, considered the patriarch of all Japanese bulldozers.

Soon, Komatsu's farm tractors and bulldozers were widely recognized around the country as technological wonders. With the addition of Komatsu's machine tools, this equipment would play a large role in a much different mission than it had during the war: the reconstruction of postwar Japan.

A Profound Belief in the Management of Change

Komatsu surged into the production of dump trucks, forklifts and hydraulic shovels, the last product being released under the name "Power Shovel," which became the generic term for all hydraulic shovels. By the 1990s, Komatsu was actually providing digital technology and peripheral gearbox devices for Formula One racing teams including Lotus and Williams, helping to raise Komatsu's reputation for world-class reliability, stability, and performance.

As of 2009, Komatsu is Asia's leading construction equipment machine maker. Globally, it is number two behind Caterpillar. Yet when Masahiro Sakane became company president, the company was 80 billion yen in the red and aching for some structural reform. Without hesitation, Sakane got to work with some swift retooling to turn his company into something capable of expanding earnings in a low-growth environment.

In addition to ordinary cost-reduction activities, one of the questions Sakane addressed was how to better detect and respond to problems in the field, primarily in the operation of construction and mining equipment. He oversaw development of a program aimed at giving everyone in the organization access to real-time data and conditions so that response could be immediately and effectively crafted. Sakane hoped to do away with complacent thinking like: "Someone will get around to doing it," or "It'll work out somehow."

That is not to say that Komatsu hadn't been vigilant about quality management. Before Sakane's presidency, Komatsu had been a pioneer and leader in *kaizen* (improvement) processes and Total Quality Management (TQM), and had in place a system for treating problems the moment they occurred. But Sakane felt it wasn't extensive enough. There were too many people who remained outside the loop. The system needed to be deployed beyond mere machinery issues and extend to anything and everything that takes place in the field, from the identification of a problem to response. What Sakane wanted everyone in the company to be able to do was visualize what was happening in the workplace through an information and fact-sharing process called "Show and Share."

Another of Sakane's reforms had to do with *kaizen* process itself, and the need to follow up on improvements and solutions to problems continually. This included gathering data on the quality of the response. How effective was it? How efficient was it? How appropriate was it? It included a thorough review of the nature of the response itself, not just in terms of its degree of effectiveness. If a division outside the field was to encounter a similar problem, it would immediately have at its fingertips plenty of information on how or how not to proceed. As a result, trial-and-error redundancies were significantly removed and work efficiency raised beyond even Sakane's expectations.

Within the short span of a single year since assuming the company's top spot, Sakane engineered a marvelous recovery that wiped out Komatsu's deficits and put it 33 billion yen in the black, overcoming the "extremely grave" situation that those around him had been whispering about behind closed doors.

"There's always a reason for the situation you're in," opines Sakane. "A reason for going into debt, a reason for becoming profitable. As a manager, you need to make a concerted effort to get at those reasons, those causes, and find out exactly what's wrong, and then diligently and patiently apply yourself to each task."

Sakane says that a manager must try at all times to be aware of what's happening in the field, and have channels of communication open so as not to overlook factors that could lead to problems in a company. Reforming an organization is, at heart, reform of the *genba*, the workplace. It is bottom up. Reforms simply won't work otherwise. Sakane says that 70 percent of added value is created at workplaces, so focusing on *genba* is what saved the company.

There are few managers who speak as passionately about the importance of knowing the workplace as Sakane:

Telling people to stick closely to the workplace is actually easier said than done. Of course, "sticking close" doesn't mean that all you have to do is be there. You need to manage your company so that anyone can visualize how it is being run, including costs. You need to have a thorough grasp of the number and status of projects underway, the work that is involved, and what subsidiaries are doing. It means having an eagle eye when it comes to understanding what state the company is in.

This is what Sakane likes to call "visualization."

If you strengthen people's visibility, they are more capable of exhibiting the wisdom and resourcefulness needed to solve problems on their own. If, on the other hand, there is a lot they feel they are not a party to, they're likely to harbor anxieties about what they themselves can achieve. So by knowing exactly where and how things relate to each other, it becomes much easier for them to see the forest for the trees and grasp where the problems lie. That, in turn, leads to quicker and more resolute action.

Questions such as: "What is the most optimal production run for a specific product?" and "What would be the best supply–demand balance?" were converted into data for everyone to grasp. Getting into the details helped paint a bigger picture for everyone, with the result being higher earnings.

Sakane took mechanisms that were already in place in the company, and simply extended them to their fullest measure. Areas of cost that had previously gone untouched got a hard look:

> There is never a good reason for doing nothing; for giving up. Before you give into a reflex urge to say, "This is an absolutely necessary expense" or "This is an unavoidable cost," I say, "If that's true, then prove it to me beyond a reasonable doubt."

The result was a reduction in fixed costs over two years that amounted to 50 billion yen. With costs significantly slashed, a healthy Komtasu seemed suddenly visible, which stoked a renewed passion toward product development. Making full use of information technology and incorporating more real-time information into decision making, Komatsu was able to give birth to a slew of new products and services unlike any it had ever produced. For example, Komatsu started installing GPS functionality and telecommunication devices into its products, enabling tracking and monitoring of in-use machinery. Komatsu could ascertain where and under what conditions a machine was being deployed, allowing for more accurate and real-time management.

In the event of malfunctions, maintenance responses would be quick and timely, and since the degree of use a machine was getting could be monitored, preventive maintenance became equally important for raising operation rates. If Komatsu equipment was viewed as having very high operational rates, companies would opt to use it more, and in greater volume, than rival products.

Sakane also worked to increase management transparency, or visualization:

> Some of the biggest problems simply lay hidden from view. People started falsely thinking that we couldn't move products when actually the problems lay not in manufacturing but in lack of visibility in other sales, marketing, and distribution. By thoroughly flushing out costs and other factors so that they

were visible, we were able then to reduce waste, redundancies, and inconsistencies. When all those downstream functions improved, we found ourselves getting back to a natural state of building strong products and improving competitiveness.

Rather than covering up weak points, they were thoroughly aired, and accompanied by an aggressive introduction of new technology such as added IT and global standardization of component manufacturing to better enable the company to compete with rivals at the highest level.

"We've come to a point where we are able to churn out highly differentiated products not seen by our competitors," says Sakane. "We can now produce components simultaneously at all production bases around the world through a system of common standards and platforms, thanks to IT support. This not only enables us to share the same values across the organization worldwide, but also eradicates time differences."

Such changes to production methods have given Komatsu greater flexibility in adjusting not only to changes in demand but also to fluctuations in costs, enabling Komatsu to alter priorities between countries dynamically down to the individual assembly line.

Generating "Dantotsu" Products

It is one thing to look at advances in IT and decide that you need to ride the current of the times, and another actually to adopt and parlay those advances into new and groundbreaking successes. Sakane believes in the importance of building equipment and services that Komatsu is uniquely positioned to build and turn into the world's best.

We call these "Dantotsu" [unique and unrivaled] products, where we concentrate our resources on building superiority into our products. Even the weakest, most "inferior" components of that product must still be at least equally competitive to those of our rivals. But it's not easy to know ahead of time precisely what a Dantotsu product is going to entail because the last thing you want to make is something superbly innovative and wonderful, but that proves to be a white elephant commercially.

For that reason, the one area that Sakane left untouched in his cost-cutting reforms was R&D, due to his firm belief that without a significant R&D budget, one's chances of producing an ideal product are slim to none:

> People have questioned my thinking on this, but I believe the first step to developing a Dantotsu product is to decide what areas we are willing to concede to our competitors. What I mean is that once we have designated those areas, we can begin to think about those aspects of a product where we can guarantee ourselves a sizable advantage for years to come.

For example, the GPS-enabled Komatsu Machine Tracking System mentioned earlier (KOMTRAX) does more than gather operational information about machines using onboard web and GPS technology. It is an asset management system that monitors operational conditions of equipment and detects malfunctions. It would take years to build a similar commercial-ready system from scratch. But rather than stopping at reaping first-to-market profits, Komatsu's strategy is to continue advancing the sophistication and practical utility of such a system to levels that cannot easily be copied. This is at the heart of a so-called "only one" strategy aimed at building products with staying power.

Create Employment Opportunities with Reform

Cost review is a vital component of any structural reform. Komatsu has not been immune from the agonizing decision to cut back on its labor force in trying times. But the Komatsu belief is that even where partial downsizing is unavoidable, the restructuring effort must serve to return the company to growth and a new stage of development that creates conditions for renewed employment.

If all one does is continue to downsize and cut costs, those actions will ultimately leave a company too thin on human talent and weakened to do battle in the next business paradigm. Sakane remains mindful that things are made by people, companies are made by people.

> I don't think there is a manager out there who takes any pleasure in restructuring. But sometimes you have no choice but to bite the bullet and make some sacrifices for the love of the

company and a belief in the company's future. Which is why it is so important that any restructuring you do be not haphazard but effective in moving the company forward to the next stage of evolution. Otherwise, the sacrifices will have been made in vain, and you will fail to gain the understanding and support of your people.

Accelerate Demand in Your Areas of Strength

Komatsu's biggest rival is of course the US-based Caterpillar company, the world's leading manufacturer of construction and mining equipment. But these two top-tier global powerhouses differ greatly in their sales strategies. Caterpillar begins by securing distribution channels through dealership networks and production bases. This is a method entailing gradual expansion of one's sphere of activities, and means the achievement of objectives can require considerable time. Early-stage results are therefore relatively slow in coming. Once a dealership distribution route is established, however, an overseas order for a component, for example, can be filled within 48 hours. In fact, 40–50 percent of Caterpillar sales come this way (as primarily maintenance service) through its dealership network.

Komatsu operates in a very different way. The company begins by aggressively selling its more affordable and easy-to-purchase lightweight construction machinery first (mainly for civil engineering works). In other words, Komatsu looks to sell its equipment over as wide an area as possible, with the hope of creating more extensive customer relationships from those point-by-point transactions.

Having earned a wide area presence and share in low-end goods, Komatsu then looks to establish bases in those areas to provide components and other construction equipment. This is a flatter and more dispersed distribution model than the dealership infrastructure of Caterpillar, but one that provides relatively quick results as more and more bases are set up in various locations around the world. Moreover, this is reinforced by IT technology to ascertain workplace conditions and by the "Genba to Komatsu" program, involving the dispatch of specially trained, on-site support staff and training workshops at key bases around the world. With such a system, horizontal connections begin somewhat weakly, but strengthen as more and more bases are built.

Caterpillar still boasts greater than twice the market share of Komatsu, and is particularly strong in Europe and North America.

But Komatsu is countering with a twofold share over Caterpillar in the high-growth markets of Asia, notably China and Russia. Given the global slowdown in 2008, much of the expected future growth in construction equipment is expected to come in Asia.

For that reason, Caterpillar, too, is working to extend its reach into Asian markets. Caterpillar had been part of a 50–50 joint venture with Mitsubishi Heavy Industries since 1963 in Mitsubishi Caterpillar Co., Ltd. But on March 26, 2008, Mitsubishi reduced its stake to 33 percent through a share redemption plan, making Caterpillar a majority shareholder in Shin Caterpillar Mistsubishi Ltd., with an option to acquire full ownership status in five years. This puts Caterpillar in prime position to carry out a comprehensive business strategy in the rapidly expanding Asian and Asia–Pacific markets. In August 2008, the company name was changed to Caterpillar Japan under a group holdings structure. Caterpillar Japan's leading products are its excavators, more popularly known as "Yumbo," offered in a wide range of sizes to suit various construction purposes large and small. Agile and highly maneuverable, Caterpillar-Mitsubishi excavators command a high share of their product category worldwide, and are expected to play an increasingly active role in construction sites across Asia.

Komatsu must further seek to manifest its uniqueness in product and service development to expand its lead in Asian markets if it hopes to keep the aggressive Caterpillar at bay.

With Caterpillar applying pressure, Sakane likes to remind his people of the many obstacles they have faced together thus far in hopes of rallying them around a united sense of action. Once he had engineered his company's V-shaped recovery, Sakane felt comfortable to begin exerting a little more of his own leadership style and philosophy. The ethical imperative he gives to his charges is to "reinforce strong points and reform weak points." Bolstering strengths, Sakane says, is just as essential to structural reform as addressing weaknesses:

> Our social mission is to maximize the efficiency of construction work under all manner of conditions, and ensure safety and stability. Conditions will differ with every field location, and with every work objective. But no matter what the country or site, we have to be ready to provide construction machinery that can respond appropriately and immediately to those needs.

Therefore, we must constantly endeavor to reinforce our strengths while simultaneously overcoming our deficiencies wherever they are found. This is not limited to our products but extends also to the people who handle our equipment.

Sakane's impassioned call to hone strengths and reform weaknesses may lie directly at the heart of what will keep Japanese manufacturing vibrant, healthy, and competitive in an era of low growth and stiff global competition. With a dwindling birth rate and an aging population at home, Japanese company survival will hinge not on productivity and output as in the past, but on differentiation and the ability to offer unique value. It is no longer sufficient to make and sell a good product at a competitive price. One must also have the flexibility and agility to deliver on a diversity of needs and wants quickly and effectively.

Summary: Primacy of the Workplace

Komatsu chairman, Masahiro Sakane, grew up in the relatively isolated prefecture of Shimane facing the Sea of Japan, removed from the major urban centers of the country and yearning for life on a busier and grander scale. He therefore attended Osaka City University and entered the workforce in 1963 amid the advent of freer movement of capital in Japan and rumors of colossal foreign corporations coming in to take over the market. All this filled Sakane with a strong competitive desire to beat these foreign concerns at their own game, since only the auto and electrical industries seemed to receive protections against foreign capital. In choosing to work for Komatsu, Sakane was motivated from the start of his career to outperform Caterpillar, or at least develop means to prevent being crushed by powerful foreign capital.

By the time Sakane became president of Komatsu in 2001, his determination to beat the world's leading bulldozer company rested on reforming the business structure and improving the company's practices of TQM, extensive and highly organized (*kaizen*) improvement activities aimed at boosting performance quality at every level to obtain higher customer satisfaction. Komatsu had been a long-time pioneer and leader in TQM for years, but this needed to be extended on a more global scale.

One by one, Sakane sought to parlay his own experiences implementing TQM as a human resource development tool reforming the value chain, described as all the activities undertaken around the world by all internal divisions from R&D, production to sales, services, and administration including external suppliers and distributors. His "quality-centered management" focused on the concept of visualization at workplaces and in business management, on communicating to all employees current conditions, ongoing challenges, trends, and expectations:

> The greater the visualization among all stakeholders the more able the company is to improve quality and reliability. So TQM is therefore applied not just to manufacturing but to accounting, HR and all other facets of corporate activity . . . *Genbaryoku* (*genba* strength) is the ability of workplaces to achieve goals and solve problems. It is a combination of policy management and daily management.

In this way, Sakane encouraged workplace improvements to be undertaken in every facet of the business and to be built upon each other until they could achieve critical mass. By the time he was finished, Sakane had put a company that was deep in debt back on a high growth track, earning Sakane the prestigious Deming Prize to honor major advances in quality improvement among Japanese companies.

In recent years, some of Japan's biggest companies have welcomed foreign leaders to manage the companies. Nissan brought in French automaker executive, Carlos Ghosn, when the two companies forged an alliance. With it has come an often controversial but patently Western-style of top-down management. Sakane once asked Ghosn, "Don't you think that what has worked to preserve the strength of Japanese manufacturing has been the strength of a middle-up, middle-down management orientation?" To which Ghosn replied, "If top down is a French style of management, then I would say my impressions of Japanese companies is that they are bottom up in orientation. But you're right, perhaps the best style of management lies somewhere in between."

Komatsu is currently working on being a global company, installing GPS systems in all of its new products so that anywhere in the world where there is a lot of work to be done, Komatsu excavators can be efficiently and effectively deployed, monitored, and maintained. As a result, it is doing that very thing in high-growth, rapid construction regions such as China, Russia, and the Middle East even as much of the world suffers from a deep recession. At the core of Komatsu's global strategy lies Sakane's "workplace primacy and visualization, and these remain at the core of the company philosophy under the stewardship and direction of current president, Kunio Noji."

Principal Ideas of Masahiro Sakane

- Strengthen "visibility" throughout your organization while honing strengths and reforming weaknesses.
- Concentrate resources on building "only one" superiority into your products and services.
- Know the workplace (*genba*), and treat the knowledge gained there as precious assets.

Komatsu Ltd.

Established: May 13, 1921

Representative: Masahiro Sakane, Chairman of the Board

Head office: 2-3-6, Akasaka, Minato-ku, Tokyo

http://www.komatsu.com/

Capital: 67,900 million yen (year ending March 2009)

Consolidated sales: 2,021,743 million yen

Consolidated operating profit: 151,948 million yen

Consolidated net profit: 78,797 million yen

Worldwide employees: 39,855

13

INCREASING MANAGEMENT QUALITY

Fujio Mitarai
Chairman and CEO
Canon Inc.

Born September 1935. Oita Prefecture, Japan. Graduated from Chuo University's Faculty of Law. That same year, he joined the company founded and run by his uncle, Takeshi Mitarai, called Canon. Became president of Canon USA in 1979. Served as a senior executive from April 1989, before being appointed the company's sixth president in 1995 after the sudden death of his cousin, Hajime, who had been president. Became chairman in 2006 as well as chairman of Nippon Keidanren (Japan Business Federation).

Breaking from a Medical Tradition

Canon Inc. is already a global leader in world-class cameras, copier machines, and office automation equipment and it claims a true master businessman in one of its founders and first president, Takeshi Mitarai.

Oddly, this soon-to-be leading industrialist was originally an obstetrician by trade. Upon graduating from Hokkaido University's medical school, Mitarai moved to Tokyo and began working for the Japan Red Cross. Before World War II, he had opened the Mitarai Obstetrics and Gynecology Hospital in Tokyo extending what had become a proud family tradition of producing medical doctors.

He became an enthusiastic supporter of and advisor to a friend's 1933 business venture to build a high-grade Japanese camera.

The company that resulted four years later was Precision Optical Industry Company and his friend was its co-founder, Saburo Uchida. Nine years later, Mitarai would find himself no longer a practicing physician but the president of a camera company. The company name was changed to "Canon Inc." in 1969, assuming the trademark title of its flagship camera products and it was two years earlier, in 1967, its thirtieth year, that the company began to diversify its business under the slogan "cameras in the right hand, business machines in the left."

Mitarai was a man who was always looking ahead, to the point where his mind seemed to dwell in a world that was not quite at hand, but just around the corner. In 1962, he was the first to introduce a five-day workweek in Japan ahead of other companies under the conviction that "family must come before work." This was a notion that seemed anathema to a country that was consumed with postwar reconstruction and catching up to the West. For someone to be admonishing people not to work themselves too hard and put family first must have seemed strangely out of step with a country that was in the midst of creating an economic miracle.

Rivals Help You Clarify Goals

What inspired Mitarai and his colleagues to build a precision instruments industry in Japan was hallowed German cameramaker, Leitz, and a camera dubbed the "father of cameras." The Leica was the pride of German technology. It was far superior to anything else on the market, boasting a rangefinder that would see military application and plenty of action in World War II.

The beauty of Leica was its highly sophisticated construction of components and block-cutting technique. Its rangefinder, ball-bearing winding mechanism, and a film loader that was ingeniously designed to preserve film planarity cemented its reputation as the only choice for professional photographers. It was "Leica or nothing." What's more, Leitz was rigorous in production quality control for its Leica and all other products, establishing a high benchmark for would-be competitors.

Yet all was not smooth sailing for Leica even as it earned a peerless reputation, for the war was not going well for Germany. Leicas, which required the assembly of many sophisticated, precision components, cost about as much as a new home. When it hit the German market, it received rave reviews, but its price was way out of reach for most people. Leicas were therefore used mostly in the filmmaking industry.

Leica cameras' unrivaled beauty and technical perfection did offer inspiration for what human technology could achieve. The finder, which used a luxurious prism, allowed in light and images with such sublime clarity that people were moved simply by looking through it; never mind its role as a camera component. From the coveted Barnack model to the M model series still in production today, Leica cameras have long occupied a lofty place in the camera firmament, even as the company has repeatedly found itself on the brink of extinction.

For Mitarai, the Leica was fuel for his ambition. His postwar goal for the company was to "catch up with, and then surpass the Leica" by building the best camera in the world.

Mitarai was eager to resume work on production of cameras after the war. But he needed the permission of the Supreme Commander of Allied Powers, General Douglas MacArthur to do it. When it was granted, Mitarai began masterminding plans to enter the American market with his proud rangefinder in hand. His brimming confidence emanated from what he believed was already better than a Leica flash diffuser and user-friendly variable magnification finder. While Leica finders were extremely sophisticated and elegant, users had to keep on hand a variety of external finders to switch in and out of the cameras depending on the type of lens used. Mitarai thought that consumers would be turned off by the extra hassle of carrying them around, not to mention the capital outlay required to acquire them.

There was another great source of excitement and pride for Mitarai: his lens. At the time, f values—which refer to lens brightness and enable photography in varying light conditions—didn't go any lower than f/2. But Canon had come out with a lens with an f value of 1.9. Here was a great opportunity for Mitarai to demonstrate that Japan possessed world-class technology.

Unfortunately, with an exchange rate fixed at 360 yen to the dollar and an economy suffering from deflation, very little was selling. That is until war broke out on the Korean peninsula. Canon saw orders of military cameras skyrocket. With some retrofitting, all of Canon's excess inventory disappeared over night, and Canon had seen its way through its first major crisis.

As Mitarai looked toward entering the looming and lucrative American market, he also began hiring and training young technicians.

Making Leica its benchmark gave Canon clear objectives. But striving to surpass Leica meant constantly seeking to raise quality standards. Slowly but surely, Canon was becoming a premium camera brand.

When the time was right for Mitarai to debut his products in the US, they were met with high marks. They had already won passionate devotees among the Allied Occupation Forces. More than a few would say they were better than Leica. But there remained one formidable barrier to overcome. Japan was still under occupation. When looking to find dealers in America, he was told, "We can't sell them as a Japanese brand. But we'll take them if we can produce them under our brand." Mitarai refused:

> Canon must launch around the world as Japanese made. I cannot rely on someone else to raise and nurture my own child.

Mitarai used his own resources to build a modern factory, and resolved to build his own sales routes and networks. Construction was completed on the new Shimomaruko Plant along the Tama River in Tokyo in 1951. At the time, Canon only had 50 million yen in capital, and needed to borrow three times that to get the site built. Many observers saw this move as complete folly.

Mitarai was determined to prove the naysayers wrong, however, and miraculously managed to pay back his debts within three years of the plant's opening in late 1954. The plant had been for Mitarai and his management team a big adventure but they had cast worries aside in favor of a fervent belief in their ambitions. Canon sales during those three years rose from 600 million yen to 1.9 billion yen.

Long before "globalization" became a corporate mantra in Japan, Mitarai had nurtured a strong desire for global success. He sent all his children to study in the US, and one son, Hajime, who would later become Canon's fifth president, graduated from MIT:

> If you're going to compete in the world, you'd do better by knowing it.

Don't Slack, Sustain the Attack

When fifth Canon president, Hajime Mitarai, died from pneumonia in 1995, the company reins passed to his cousin, Fujio Mitarai. Canon did not as a matter of policy seek to maintain the Mitarai line of succession at the top, but Fujio seemed to have both the pedigree and the talent to lead.

Fujio Mitarai has so far lived up to the billing, making a name for himself as a savvy business leader who saw the need for introducing stronger cash-flow management and strengthening the company's balance sheet. While his predecessor, Hajime, had really helped turn Canon into one of the world's most innovative electronics manufacturers, it was Fujio who got down to the nitty-gritty business of streamlining what had become an overextended organization. He pulled the company quickly out of the liquid crystal display, optical disc, and personal computer businesses. He concentrated personnel and management resources on the company's core competencies and strengths in cameras, copier–printers, and semiconductor manufacturing equipment.

Specifically, Fujio got to work overhauling production and development departments, for example, completely replacing the conveyor belt method with cell-based production:

> The advantage of cell production is that once you have proficiency in it, productivity rises dramatically. While you have to begin with the involvement of many people, within six months to a year, you only need half as many people to produce the same quality levels as before. As soon as we switched to cell production, we could get rid of conveyor belts that lay idle on their sides in the plants. Believe it or not, that alone freed up about 20 baseball stadiums worth of work space.

Mitarai regarded this as the 1 + 1 = 3 or 4 production equation.

These efforts to "reform the ground under you" paid off in a healthier balance sheet. Consolidated earnings grew from just over two trillion yen in 1995 to 3.5 trillion yen in 2004. Pretax profits swelled sixfold, from more than 100 billion yen in 1995 to 600 billion yen in 2005. Much of the earnings were then used to pay off debt, demonstrating Fujio's belief and acumen in fiscal discipline.

A few years ago, Fujio Mitarai explained his strategy at a public press conference:

> In the few years since the turn of the millennium, we have seen nothing less than a complete transformation in the global economic landscape. Asian productivity is rising dramatically, and world markets are flooded with cheaper goods. We're about

to face great excess supply on a global scale. In the future, I think we can predict globalization of markets to continue and an environment very vulnerable to deflationary trends. This deflation is unavoidable.

To address this developing paradigm best, Mitarai explained that Canon really has no choice but to defend its brand by seeking profit growth in high value-added products and services that cannot be made in China or other parts of Asia, and don't rely on increased production or sales volume.

Mitarai has on several occasions stressed how China will become the next great market for the high value-added manufactured goods of Japanese companies. Like Canon's first president, Takeshi Mitarai, Fujio believes a strong overseas strategy to be indispensable. Canon is planning to expand its brand overseas with great expectations that the size of BRIC economies will exceed those of the G7 nations by 2050. Mitarai aims to build products that will be cherished and appreciated, and a company that is held in the highest esteem the world over:

> There are two major currents up ahead. One is to foster globalization without changing conventional ways, and the other is to go broadband.

"Going broadband" refers to the onslaught of moving image functionality that will be made available in key digital products such as the company's EOS single-lens reflex cameras:

> The world is definitely moving from an age of still to moving images. In tandem with IT advances, networks are also evolving quickly. An environment of greater network functionality, display performance, new and added value, and the means to enjoy all of that, is what lies ahead.

All the new technologies will be easily deployed in people's living rooms through new solutions.

Mitarai's Canon will focus more on its areas of value-added expertise and strive for top player status in peripheral segments outside of cameras, including multifunction devices and other office imaging systems, semiconductor exposure systems and LCD exposure systems, television lenses, and other industrial equipment, not to mention a new area for Canon in digital X-ray cameras and DNA testing systems:

> This will require strengthening R&D, and we plan to ratchet our R&D budget up over the next decade from 275 billion yen in '04 to 500 billion yen, of which 200 billion will be allocated to basic research.

Sustain Efforts to Innovate and Evolve

In the face of a deepening global economic crisis, Canon has dubbed 2009 as the year of "Improved Management Quality."

"These tough times present a golden opportunity to bolster our corporate structure," Mitarai and his management team write in the company's global website. "We are undertaking a major course change for Phase III of the Excellent Global Corporation Plan, launched in 2006, from sound growth to improved management quality."

Canon's phased "Excellent Global Corporation Plan" was launched in 1996 to be executed over five years. By the mid-to-late 1990s, the business division system was beginning to show signs of fatigue and unwieldiness. Plus the company held over 840 billion yen in debt.

There was a dire need for some systemic changes. It had to start with the balance sheet. Fujio's appointment as the sixth Canon company president became the turning point for launching a reform initiative that would seek to overhaul the company's finances and firmly establish Canon's leadership in the world. It was a long-term business reform plan to be carried out in phases.

The first phase was slated for 1996–2000. Phase I was to center on profits and "total optimization." It was consciousness reform, and a period in which financial standing would be bolstered through better cash flow management and "selection and concentration" of business areas. Phase II, 2001–05, was to be a time spent bolstering competitive strength, by keeping its eyes on changing demand while aggressively promoting digitalization of product lines under the banner of becoming global leader in all major business areas where Canon operates.

Phase III would take place from 2006 to 2010. As of 2009 when this book was written, Canon is focusing on sound growth in next-generation technologies and establishing new production methods while strengthening supply chain management and other areas of corporate management. Upon completing this phase, Canon hopes to find itself ranked among the world's top 100 companies.

Canon has identified next-generation businesses in the areas of "medical imaging," "intelligent robotics" and "safety" fields, where synergies and commonalities can be found through Canon technologies. Along with promoting a deepening of industrial–academic co-development with universities and leading research institutions around the world, Canon is looking to strengthen state-of-the-art technology in its specialty fields such as high-performance sensors.

To ensure stable and improved production of Canon's high-quality products, Canon needs to create new production methods that can give it a globally competitive edge. What will be required is establishment of fully automated lines (automation machinery and robots) for design, production, and manufacturing technologies to form three legs of the stool.

When Phase III ends in 2010, Canon hopes to lead the world, overwhelmingly, in all of its core businesses.

Fujio Mitarai stepped down from day-to-day management in May of 2006, naming Tsuneji Uchida as his replacement president and COO. Mitarai maintained his CEO title and became chairman of both Canon and the Keidanren. Uchida reiterated his commitment to Canon's ongoing Excellent Global Corporation Plan:

> When the end of Phase III comes around in 2010, we plan not so much to be in a lot of segments but to have expanded our horizons in existing businesses and in new product areas that skew to slightly different markets than before.
>
> For example, we have long had great strength in sensor technology. Based on that, we can reduce the size of our sensors to help in the development of robotics with highly sophisticated movements and functionality, which also allows us to reduce reliance on heavy human labor by boosting robotic automation in the manufacturing processes of our own products.
>
> We are also expanding our printing technology for professional use. This represents a movement into a new field for us. While we developed and sold consumer products such as our inkjet printers to great success, on a market-share basis, it would be difficult to win in that space alone. So we thought, "Why not take the technology we're good at and look to build that into new

application areas?" That led to the birth of a new market for multifunction products and digital presses to meet the needs of small-scale businesses or printers who seek high-end printing at small print runs.

Canon also offers networking through personal computers for each of its products. Currently, this can be done through wireless LAN, USB, and various flash memory card media, for which Canon employs its own proprietary technology enabling all types of data to be processed on all products.

For example, the full high-definition moving picture data housed in EOS digital single-lens reflex cameras, one of Canon's flagship products, can be used across all of Canon's product platforms and digital equipment easily.

By the end of 2008, 30 percent of Canon's total sales came from the consumer product market, but the company has not changed its stance that the industrial application sphere must be built upon support and success in the general consumer sphere. This added networking capability is premised on the consistent idea at Canon that products should continually be made more useful for the general consumer.

Moreover, one cannot overlook that nearly 10 percent of all sales are allocated to research and development of new products and new technologies. Conventionally, competitor companies in the same field allocate about 6 percent of revenues to R&D. Never being satisfied with the success of current products, Canon strives to carve out its own destiny through its "3 Selfs" spirit. These are "self-motivation," "self-management," and "self-awareness." "Self-motivation" means taking a proactive, self-motivated approach to everything. "Self-management" refers to taking personal responsibility. "Self-awareness" urges a constant mindfulness of one's role and stance, and being able to grasp changing situations and conditions.

Behind the large ambition to win an overwhelming global share of the markets Canon participates in, says Uchida, is a serious and uncompromising effort to address down-to-earth values to help guide the individual employee:

We're working hard every day with the goal of becoming number one in all our business areas, but we're not there yet in every area. We believe we can get there if we keep working tirelessly at it. In those areas where we are already the global leader, we have to maintain a vigilant mentality and keep the pressure on, continuing to work hard to sustain our competitive edge.

To earn that global number one position, Uchida might first focus on Canon's mainstay product, the EOS digital camera (digital AF single-lens reflex camera). But here he stresses the need to actively invest in all of Canon's endeavors and encourage a sustained effort, through trial-and-error, to develop the best sensor technology, lenses and even software, all the while ensuring these processes are supervised by tight quality control.

Finally, Uchida points to sustaining a solid consensus among all involved and working toward a common goal—becoming the world's best—as being of primary importance.

Communicate to Inspire

"If you want to move a company in the right direction, communication is everything," says Mitarai:

This naturally means encouraging a healthy exchange of opinion in each section and division of your organization, which includes clarifying objectives and providing ideas for how you want them achieved. Only when you have all of this flowing together can you begin to see good results. Advancements in telecommunications and shipping technologies have really improved communications, particularly with people overseas. The internet allows for effortless interaction. You can get your message out to the world through blogs and websites. As long as you have a clear idea of what you want, gathering and conveying information can be done with ease. So there really is no excuse for not using these resources effectively.

Traveling abroad, too, has become so much easier than in the past. When I was a college student, it took me 26 hours just to go from my native home in Oita to Tokyo. But now in half that time, I can travel to New York or London. Travel is no longer so costly. So I recommend and think it is very meaningful to put yourself in a different environment while you're still young, and meet people who live by different norms and values than you.

Although the availability of tools have made communication easier, it is incumbent upon individuals to make the effort to become active members of our global society. If you aren't accessible to the world, you won't earn any respect. If you want to achieve success globally with "made in Japan" products, it is your capabilities as an individual that will be measured.

The tone of Canon's forward march will therefore be set by a leader who can set clear targets, and then earn the support of every employee toward achieving them.

Summary: Reaffirming a Japanese Style

On March 11, 2009, at a meeting to explain management direction, Canon chairman and CEO Fujio Mitarai reiterated his resolve to make Canon a truly global company, emphasizing the need to raise competitive strength of products and profitability amid shrinking global markets:

> The business environment is extremely tough right now. But we are working to improve management quality and processes to enable us to make the next big leap forward in our development as we aim to be a company that can grow and prosper over the next 100, even 200, years.

Mitarai, Canon president from 1995–2006 and now chairman and CEO, pointed with pride to the strong earnings his company had achieved under the Excellent Global Corporation Plan. But even Canon could not be immune from the global economic slowdown that washed over the world in the fall of 2008. After a string of record profits, Canon watched its earnings plummet.

Yet Canon is one major Japanese company that continues to defend the traditionally Japanese business practice of lifetime employment, while applying strong cash-flow and supply chain metrics to its management. It is the idea of *wakon yosai*, combining Western learning with a Japanese spirit in management. The leaders at Canon hope it will form the backbone for the ongoing evolution of the company and spirit of reform needed to ride out the current crisis and many more to come:

> The ideal is to put out a continuous, uninterrupted string of products that satisfy consumer demands. But if you're going to make high value-added products at great cost performance,

you're going to have to lower cost ratios to maintain business profitability. That is why we are working to unify production information systems and digitalize design. It is particularly in tough times that we must reform production using IT and polish up our cost competitiveness.

Canon president and COO, Tsuneji Uchida, drove home this point during an interview with the *Nihon Keizai* newspaper in June 2009. Uchida is widely recognized as the man inside Canon who rose from the camera division, build the world's strongest digital camera line, and advanced the "digital print age" by tying together digital cameras and inkjet printers.

"A lot of people are working hard to put out low-cost products that target emerging markets," Uchida continued. "But Canon has no plans to change its strategy of producing high-end, value-added products it has come to be known for. If demand for low-cost products grows, by extension so too will there be an eventual rise in consumers who want higher performance, higher resolution products. Sales continue to be robust in the global market for digital single-lens reflex cameras, because they have shown to be relatively immune to economic swings. That is because the needs of consumers who want to leave behind copies of their works in high resolution have not abated. If we continue to make products that respond to those needs, they will sell even in bad economic times."

Although Canon saw a contraction and rapid decline in demand for its flagship digital cameras from autumn 2008, Uchida is confident that customers will be returning, and Canon will be there to respond with its sophisticated, value-added products.

The roots of this loyal dedication and commitment to highly individualized craftmanship dates back to 1933 and the ambition of Takeshi Mitarai, a young obstetrician and trained engineer who, burning with a desire to outperform German cameramaker, Leica, helped establish a luxury camera factory called the Precision Optical Instruments Laboratory. The very next year, Japan's first domestically made, luxury 35-millimeter camera debuted in prototype form: the "Kwanon."

Named after the highly revered Buddhist *bodhisattva* of mercy in Japan, Kwanon (in Japanese), the "Canon" brand immediately made believers of customers as a high-end camera soon after World War II. The next big landmark product came in 1976 with the world's first single-lens reflex camera to house a microcomputer, the AE-1. It proved a huge hit in the US, and helped Canon become a globally recognized brand. Founding president Takeshi Mitarai brandished an ideal not only to "build the world's best camera," but to do so in a company atmosphere with a creed built on three principles that stressed ability (merit), health, and family, and behavioral guidelines called the "3 Selfs" spirit: "self-motivation, "self-management," and "self-awareness."

Mitarai viewed the family as the fundamental spiritual unit of human life, and this formed the keystone for a Canon corporate culture that cherishes people. Current Canon chairman and CEO Fujio Mitarai, nephew of the first president, spent 23 years in the US, starting in 1966 when he traveled to New York to work at the headquarters of Canon USA—a time during which he also studied American business and brought home American-style rational business practices to incorporate into Canon's Japanese business methods. Since then, Canon has been built upon a unique fusion of two business philosophies, a concept expressed in the word *kyosei*, which is also the term used to describe Canon's philosophy of creating a world of coexistence, mutual prosperity, and growth among all peoples.

Canon looked ahead and saw that a business organized to rely on the sale of cameras alone would be shortlived, and from the 1960s began diversifying into products such as copiers. Management, too, diversified. The oil crisis of 1973 brought stiffer competition, during which Canon had to deal with a defective component in one of its pocket calculator products. This became a valuable lesson for Canon, which would craft its "Excellent Global Corporation" reform concept to strengthen fiscal discipline, R&D, and human resources.

When in 1977 a new president came into office in Ryuzaburo Kaku, he instantly raised the company's R&D budget from 4–5 percent of sales to 10 percent, and strengthened its staff. It has stayed about that level ever since.

Kaku converted the company's technology to intellectual property rights such as patents, creating the precedent for today's model of company growth with technology as a driving force. The result was a flurry of new product development leading to the introduction of a division-based structure in the company and expansion of those divisions into printers, fax machines, and personal computers.

The Plaza Accords of 1985, which sparked a sudden increase in the value of the yen, contributed to the rise of unprofitable divisions at Canon. The mounting red ink exposed many problems with the division-based system and its diluted head office controls.

Enter Fujio Mitarai, who upon his return from the US in 1989 took up a senior executive position in the company and set about a program to streamline management. When he was named president in 1995, Mitarai laid out a long-term consolidated management and profitability-centered, cash-flow plan as core pillars of a turnaround effort, and undertook a large-scale business overhaul that pulled Canon out of nonperforming business sectors, including production of personal computers. This would set the stage and lay the foundation for the company's high earnings management in the years to come.

But beginning in the autumn of 2008, as the global economy fell into a deep recession, nearly 10 years of continuous growth and record-breaking earnings came to an abrupt end. Canon's policy for riding out the crisis had to be positioned on a steadfast defense of its traditional corporate culture and values: continue to apply an uncompromising value-added management approach to building good products.

In 2009, in the company's first president's home city of Oita, Kyushu, Canon launched the Oita Manufacturing Training Center, a training facility aimed at letting seasoned Canon engineers and technicians pass on to the younger generations hands-on training and know-how in the operation of various machine tools including lathes, milling machines, lens-polishing techniques, and automation devices; with the facility is also being used as a training center for acquiring the "Job Card" accreditation promoted by the Japanese government. Canon's framework for encouraging engineers to acquire patents for their inventions is famously known as the "Canon patent brigade," and in 2008, Canon was third in the world with the number of registered patents it held in the US at 2,114, and is number one in Japan in registered patents.

Although Canon operates a strong copier production facility in China, high-value-added products are still made in Japan for a divided production system. In high-end digital cameras, for example, production is done at home with most of the R&D and production of key devices such as image sensors occurring in Japan.

Canon is aiming to be a leading global company, but with its core production base still in Japan. Canon continues to hold firm to its belief in maintaining a policy at home of lifetime employment due to a conviction that the inheritance and advancement of its technological assets as well as the maintenance of high quality standards are integrally linked to high levels of cooperation among employees, not to mention cooperation with local governments and communities. Even in the most tumultuous of times, Canon is one company that does not plan to abandon its roots in a Japanese style of management.

Principal Ideas of Fujio Mitarai and Tsuneji Uchida

- Concentrate on where you can add value and then strive to be the best in that space.
- Be tireless in effort and uncompromising in improving management quality.
- Uphold the "3 Selfs" spirit of self-motivation, self-management and self-awareness.

Canon Inc.

Established: August 10, 1937
Fujio Mitarai, Chairman and CEO
Tsuneji Uchida, President and COO
Head office: 3-30-2, Shimomaruko, Ohta-ku, Tokyo
http://www.canon.com/
Capital: 174,800 million yen (year ending Dec. 2008)
Consolidated sales: 4,094,161 million yen
Consolidated operating profit: 496,074 million yen
Consolidated net profit: 309,148 million yen
Worldwide employees: 166,980

14

RETURNING TO ONE'S ROOTS

Akio Toyoda
President and CEO
Toyota Motor Corp.

Born May 1956 in Nagoya, Aichi Prefecture. Graduated from Keio University in 1979, joined Toyota Motor Corporation in 1984. Established online auto information website, Gazoo.com in 1998. Served as managing director of Toyota, then senior managing director before becoming vice president in 2005. Named president in 2009. Akio is the son of sixth Toyota president Shoichiro Toyoda.

From Textiles to Automobiles

Toyota Motor Corporation, the world's largest auto company, traces its roots to a spinning loom. Founder Sakichi Toyoda, known to most as a prolific inventor, was really a carpenter by trade as his father before him. But Sakichi had a life-changing experience in 1890 when he caught a glimpse of a weaving machine, while attending a Tokyo job fair and was thoroughly captivated by the device's sophisticated construction. Sakichi studied the loom as best as he could, scratching out a quick blueprint before hurrying back to his country home in Aichi Prefecture brimming with ideas and eager to immediately begin work on a loom of his own.

Where foreign-made looms used metal, Sakichi chose wood. As a carpenter, it was the building medium with which he was most comfortable, and the prohibitive cost of metal made the option moot. Applying his carpentry mind and skill set, Sakichi built his loom completely out of wood and thought it the better for it.

He turned out to be right. By foregoing metal for more affordable wood, Sakichi was actually able to reduce the total number of parts, which in the end he deemed superfluous. The result was a device that could be produced at a tenth of the cost of foreign-made looms.

Sakichi named it the "Toyoda Man-Powered Wood Loom" and took it down to the local port, where it met with great praise and sold immediately. All in all, it was a quiet and humble exercise in diligence and ingenuity that would prove providential. Sakichi's need to reduce waste in the process would furthermore come to define a "Toyota production method" that would live on and flourish as the lifeblood of Toyota Motor Corporation for generations.

In 1929, Sakichi's son, Kiichiro, had just returned from an overseas trip aimed at giving him a firsthand look at auto industries in the US and Europe. Like Sakichi's attraction to the loom years before, Kiichiro had been irresistibly drawn to the automobile, and swore that he was going to build a successful automobile division in a corner of the Toyota Loom Works factory, and do it without relying on anyone's help. The "help" was an indictment of his father's weaving loom company, which had become a highly successful and profitable business but had to turn to a major trading company for support during a period of financial crisis. That proved to be a fateful decision for the independently minded Sakichi, who eventually found himself at odds with the rational ways of a big business and became marginalized from his own company.

This had a profound effect on Kiichiro, who vowed that he alone would procure all the money he needed for his auto division, including equipment, technology, and even staff. He knew he was asking a lot of himself, having seen what was required in the US and Europe. This was a capital-intensive venture, and Kiichiro knew he would have to be cunning, committed, and resourceful.

Indeed, just about everyone around him regarded Kiichiro's idea as preposterous. "Who could possibly compete with the likes of GM and Ford?" griped even representatives of major Japanese conglomerates such as Mitsui, Mitsubishi, and Sumitomo. Sure, Toyota had made a name for itself in weaving machines, and was already a giant of Japanese industry. But automobiles were an altogether different proposition.

Kiichiro chose not to listen. He even approached Ford with an idea for a joint venture to build trucks. Secretly, he desired to gain access to Ford's automotive production technology while still maintaining enough of a distance to protect the company from a takeover.

This idea, too, met with stiff opposition, particularly from the Japanese government, which was growing more militant and anti-American by the day. When the idea for a joint venture with Ford fizzled, those around Kiichiro assumed that he would at last "awaken from his silly dream." Few expected that Kiichiro's resolve would only grow stronger.

"I have to build automobiles," he was heard to exclaim, and if he couldn't get right down to doing so, he would spend his time learning everything he could about Western automotive technology.

One person Kiichi could count on for support, however, was his own father, Sakichi. Seeing the frustration mounting in his son, Sakichi at one point put his arm on Kiichi's shoulder and said, "Son, I invented the weaving loom, and it became a national asset [under the patent system of the time]. I received quite a bit of money from that. But what made me proudest was that I did a great service to this country. So go build your automobile. Do it for yourself, and do it for your country."

Kiichiro is said to have mentioned these words from his father years later when he felt it would help rally the support and cooperation of his Toyota employees and doubters around him. Kiichiro needed to be able to count on their passion and sacrifice to build Japan's first automobile. At the time, the world was roiled in the Great Depression. When Toyota did succeed in rolling out the first Model A1 automobile and G1 truck in 1934, the sense of jubilation was reported to be so high inside the company that "all the troubles of the world seemed to melt away."

It was again providential that Kiichiro's passion had been sparked by the automobile. But it might just as easily been something else. For Kiichiro had gradually come to realize that if his father's company was to continue to grow, it would eventually have to start building more than just weaving looms. Textiles had become a saturated industry. Toyota would need to begin thinking about building new types of machines that the domestic market would want. The automobile was just the thing, he thought.

Toyota as Its Own Worst Enemy

In August 1937, Kiichiro's dream of building a small passenger car with Japanese technology that would sell in markets around the world led to his establishing the Toyota Motor Company as an independent concern. But that dream was put on hold by the outbreak of the Pacific War. When the war ended, development of a "people's" car resumed, but Kiichiro would never see its completion. He died in March 1952. It fell to new president Taizo Ishida, technology division founder Eiji Toyoda, and others who had worked closely with Kiichiro to fulfill his dream. In 1955, they succeeded when they rolled out the Toyota Crown. It was an unqualified hit. In 1957, the Toyota brand began to make news around the world. The Crown was entered in the rigorous 10,560-mile Australian Rally, and subsequently placed third among foreign entries, marking the company's entry in international motor sports competition.

Then in 1962, as domestic sales of the Crown topped a million units, Toyota also put out the smaller "Corona" and light truck "Toyoace," and the 800cc "Publica." If the Crown represented a hop, and the Corona and Publica a step, then the jump to top automaker status would come with Eiji Toyoda's pet project, the Corolla. From the outset of development, Eiji was intent on creating an automotive revolution:

> From hereon, we need to start making cars that can compete with those of the West. Mark my words, the next car we make will spark the motorization of our country.

Eiji Toyoda's words proved prescient. The Corolla rolled out in 1965. It had an 1100cc engine—upgraded from the original plan of 1000cc—and sold for 432,000 yen (about $1,400 at the time) in a standard version and 495,000 ($1,600) in a deluxe version. That placed it several hundreds of dollars higher than the popular Nissan Sunny. But the extra kick it got from an added 100cc helped send sales skyrocketing.

The Corolla has undergone dozens of model changes since and is still produced today. More than 32 million Toyota Corollas have been sold to date, truly establishing it as the "people's car" that Kiichiro Toyoda had envisioned, and putting it alongside the Model-T Ford and Volkswagen Beetle as one of the most iconic and seminal industrial products of the twentieth century. It would be the Corolla that would set Toyota on its remarkable path to global leadership in the auto industry.

Toyota took to applying and forwarding automotive technology with a level of uncompromising passion and tireless diligence that has come to symbolize the Japanese work ethic. Add to that a deep-seated desire to improve continually upon a work or a process while weeding out the bad, and the result is a practice the world has come to know, admire, and mimic as *kaizen* (improvement). It is one thing to receive know-how from someone or somewhere else. But one doesn't truly own a creation until one has invested one's own blood, sweat, and tears into building it. That is when success is self made. When Toyota was still "floundering at the feet" of auto companies like Ford and GM, it was experiencing its own lengthy and painful process of trial and error, trying to figure out on its own the best way to make something of lasting value. If Kiichiro's planned joint venture with Ford had come to pass, he may have never built a company that would one day be regarded as the best in the world.

No sooner had Toyota climbed to the top of the global auto industry when whispers were heard that "Toyota had become its own worst enemy." It was the company's eighth president and current chairman, Hiroshi Okuda, who was doing the whispering. He wanted to warn his people against the arrogance and complacency that can set in once one feels there are no mountains left to climb.

As a model for business the world over, teams of managers were coming to Toyota to see and learn its hallowed production system and absorb its culture. Books were being written about *lean production*, *kaizen*, and *just-in-time manufacturing*. Okuda realized that each and every Toyota employee would need to start viewing the company, and his or her place in it, from the perspective of a competitor. The employees should place themselves on the outside looking in to gain a fresh perspective; look for chinks in the armor or a competitive edge to exploit. It was a psychology of vigilance that would prove vital in ensuring that what had become such an enormous and ubiquitous company could still function as though it were not.

"At every opportunity," Okuda recalls, "I would instruct Toyota employees to walk on the far side of the road, literally. I didn't want them to develop a swagger. One must always endeavor to be humble."

In an industry where fortunes are so often at the mercy of external conditions, be it crude oil prices, volatile exchange rates, or, in the case of autumn 2008, a global recession, any swagger is bound to be shortlived. So powerful was the downturn in its initial impact that only one of the "Big Three" auto giants of the US, Ford, would survive. GM and Chrysler would both have to be salvaged by either the government or outside capital help. Toyota watched a record-high operating profit of 2.27 trillion yen in 2007 dissolve into an operating loss for fiscal 2008 of 461 billion yen, and forecast that figure to swell to 850 billion yen in fiscal 2009.

A Rediscovery of Roots

On Thursday, June 25, 2009, Toyota's new president met with the press for the first time. He was Akio Toyoda, the son of honorary chairman Shoichiro Toyoda and scion of the Toyota family bloodline. Akio is a grandson of Kiichiro. His appointment captured the attention of the world. The founding family was back in power, and once again looking to re-establish the Toyota cachet amid an unprecedented crisis: Toyota was operating in the red for the first time.

Akio is actually the youngest Toyota president. His uncle, Tatsuro Toyoda, had to step down in 1995 because of illness, and was the last family member to head the company. The next three presidents would be Hiroshi Okuda, Fujio Cho, and Katsuaki Watanabe, all of whom retain advisory or chairmanship positions in the company today. But amid the first posted annual losses for the automaker in 59 years, Akio Toyoda has been tapped to lead the company toward an uncertain future, the symbolism of which has not been lost on observers.

Akio faces tremendous pressure. At his first press conference, he spoke in somber tones, his face stern. Everyone in attendance could see the great weight he bore:

> The automotive industry around the world is confronted with an enormous challenge. It is one that, regrettably, will result in Toyota posting losses for this fiscal year that are even greater than last year's. It feels like we are a boat being tossed in a storm. But we will continue to focus on the workplace [*genba*], and serve the local communities in which we reside and operate. The customer come first. We will not default on our commitment to *genchi genbutsu* [the concept of going out and seeing the world for yourself].
>
> As long as each and everyone of us in the Toyota Group continues to interact with customers and communities honestly and with the firm conviction that we will ride out this crisis, I am confident that Toyota can emerge stronger than ever before.

There is, however, some good news amid all the strife. The new-generation Prius, Toyota's dedicated gas-electric hybrid car, was released in May 2009 and received orders for 180,000 units in its first month. Benefiting from government tax breaks offered to purchasers of low-emission cars, the Prius is once again a bestseller. In the case of a new Prius, the subsidy is close to $4,000.

One well-publicized achievement by Akio Toyoda is that as an executive vice president, he was instrumental in driving down the price of the Prius from the initially projected 2.5 million yen price tag to 2.05 million yen, earning him strong praise from dealerships and consumers in the lower income regions of Japan.

"Perhaps this is a sign of bigger changes to come," commented one middle manager at Toyota.

Akio does come into the presidency with a reputation as a forward-looking manager with a fresh and objective outlook on his own company.

The Secret to Building Great Cars

Although Akio has yet to provide any real specifics about what type of management policy he plans to employ, he has stated a desire to remain as close to the *genba* as possible.

For example, on April 23, 2009, the new Toyota chief took part in the Nurburgring 24-hour endurance race in Germany as a Toyota team driver, taking two laps in the V10 sport coupe, Lexus LF-A. He wanted to get behind the wheel himself and race a car around a track to experience personally and demonstrate to the world the thrill of driving "a great car."

Whether viewed as clues into his personal character or simply as high-profile marketing, Akio's words and deeds are sure to attract a lot of attention in the days and months ahead.

Toyota finds itself once again standing on new ground wondering how to build the next great car that will re-establish its bearings for the future. But it has been in this position before, most recently with the launch of the Lexus brand in 1989, followed by the dedicated gas-electric hybrid vehicle, the Prius. The company continues to win over consumers and earn mindshare with both Lexus and the Prius, which are selling well despite plummeting auto sales around the world.

As the global recession in 2008–09 worsened, demand for the Prius actually grew stronger, with buyers having to wait several months for delivery. Production lines were ramped up to run day and night, even during the ordinarily quiet summer months. Meanwhile, orders for the first Lexus HS 250h gas-electric hybrid topped 10,000 units in its first month of release, a number 20 times higher than Toyota's original projected first-month target of 500 units. The Lexus HS 250h engine was built to get a jaw-dropping 55 miles to the gallon, essentially giving consumers the fuel efficiency of a compact car in a $40,000 luxury vehicle.

Consumer and government support for both the Lexus brand and the Prius has continued to grow since their arrival on the market. But their stories differ significantly. The Lexus idea emerged out of a steady trial-and-error process by the Toyota development team to regain technological ground it felt it was losing as emissions restrictions were relaxed in the 1980s. Toyota was also yearning to devise a strategy that could get it around tough import restrictions in the US market. The high-end segment seemed the right answer.

The prevailing reputation of Toyota in the US was that it "built high-quality but cheap cars." While that might seem the perfect formula, it translated into razor-thin margins for Toyota and its distributors. Selling on volume was therefore critical to success. But once the yen began to rise and the US government imposed heavier restrictions on imports, this model lost its viability. Toyota felt it had to move before it was too late, and so Toyota management made the decision to enter the high-margin luxury car market.

The Lexus initiative began by aiming for the performance of German luxury auto brands like Mercedes-Benz and BMW, but combined with distinctively Japanese levels of quality and reliability. *And* at the lowest price points possible. In short, the vehicle had to have all the performance and hallmarks of a luxury car, but be within reasonable reach of a greater number of consumers. Despite these ambitious and almost contradictory aims, the stiffness of the challenge galvanized the development team around what it saw as "clear and worthwhile" objectives.

But Toyota was also confronted with growing public criticism. Many saw Toyota as a self-absorbed company that cared only about its own unchecked growth with little or no regard for the world at large. This was terribly upsetting to Toyota's eighth president, Hiroshi Okuda, who was very sensitive to the attack, particularly since he was a staunch believer in the management imperative that a company grow "in harmony with society."

Okuda decided that a clean-car project would be needed to help drive his management reforms and promote a more socially conscious company. There were still no mandated standards for controlling CO_2 at the time, but global warming and greenhouse gases were serious enough global issues for Okuda to predict that mandated restrictions were imminent. The industry as a whole had long envisioned an automotive future weaned off reliance on fossil fuels and powered by cleaner forms of energy, such as electricity or hydrogen fuel cells. But the technology and infrastructure needed were still viewed as being at least 20 years away.

Okuda therefore decided to throw his company's technological weight behind development of a "hybrid" car housing an electric motor and gasoline engine that would drive cleaner and more fuel efficiently than most cars on the road. Again, this idea was far from new. But most rival automakers saw hybrid technology as merely an "interim" technology that would prove unpopular, unprofitable, and shortlived once fuel-cell and other advanced technologies came to fruition.

Taking all these factors into account, anyone could see the risk was considerable. Any forerunning endeavor is. But fortunately, Toyota's risk had been slightly mitigated by an inhouse project that was already under way to build a super fuel-efficient vehicle for the twenty-first century. It ultimately evolved into a gas-electric hybrid car concept out of a necessity to achieve the fuel-efficiency targets the project had set from its beginning. It was therefore a project that grew more revolutionary as it evolved. Now the only worry was whether Toyota could get the vehicle out on the market quickly enough to reap first-mover benefits. Honda, too, was developing a two-seater hybrid car.

When the Prius finally did arrive, ahead of schedule, it was a monumental hit that exceeded everyone's expectations. Hiroshi Okuda had delivered on his promise to raise Toyota's image as a company seeking greater harmony with society.

Toyota will again need to dip into its rich repository of ideas and resources and do something bold and new. Perhaps the relatively young Akio is just the person to elicit such a change. Cost remains a major problem. Good cars require quality materials. The better the car, the more costly it is to produce. But in a global recession, luxury car building is no longer possible. It is costly simply to procure the materials required. While it is not unreasonable to expect demand for luxury cars to return, particularly in the emerging BRIC countries, nobody can say for sure how many years that recovery will take. Even with a strong balance sheet, sitting around waiting for the sun to come out and "relying on the Toyota Bank" is simply not prudent.

In this respect, perhaps Toyota will need to make a shift to producing "low-cost, small cars" to raise revenues—something it has not done much of in recent memory. The Prius may be a strong-selling product but it alone cannot carry the company.

"It is a time to return to our roots," said Akio at the press conference to announce his presidency.

If anything signals the formation of a management philosophy, it is this phrase, which he has uttered on several occasions. But what are the roots he is talking about? For years, Toyota has been obsessed with numbers; the number of vehicles it produces and sells in nearly every auto segment and market around the world. That obsession has driven the automaker to world leadership in several categories. What Akio Toyota is talking about, however, is to return to the roots of the *monozukuri* way of thinking. *Monozukuri* often resists a proper Western rendering, but in short, it connotes a craftsperson-like attitude toward building things, in which quality and attention to detail reign as the supreme values. Production volume is not an inherent aim of the *monozukuri* mindset.

"Numbers don't come first. The individual customer and community do. So I also want to stress the need to recover our founding spirit," Akio added.

In the same way that Kiichiro sought to mobilize support among his people, Akio returns to the directive Sakichi Toyoda gave his son when he slapped him on the shoulder and told him to "go build cars for the country."

Toyota has lived through war, oil shocks, high exchange rates, pollution scandals, and trade frictions, to name just a few of its past challenges. Through each of those trials, employees have banded together under a consistent message and abiding spirit to make Toyota the number one auto company in the world. In Akio Toyoda, it is that much easier to resummon the spirit of the founder, and remind everyone of the successes that have brought them to this point.

The "strong car" that Akio will aim to produce, if based on the declaration he made to bring the company back to profitability by the end of March 2011, will need to take concrete shape within a year or two. Most likely, it will be an automobile high in environmental value; perhaps one that can travel close to 95 miles on a gallon of gas.

Although Toyota has fallen into the red for the first time in 59 years to the tune of 50 billion yen, it remains the face of Japanese industry. The company's way of doing business has been studied by just about every other Japanese business, large and small. One entrepreneur who, along with the Toyodas, helped set new standards of strong business practices in modern Japan is Konosuke Matsushita, founder of Panasonic (see chapter 10).

Toyota and Panasonic have a long shared history. For example, it used to be customary for newly promoted executives at Matsushita Electric Industries (Panasonic) to be sent to Toyota for factory tours and lectures by then Toyota president Taizo Ishida. Ishida was idolized among Panasonic employees as the "Business Master," even as they had their own "master" to look up to.

By naming Akio Toyoda as president, Toyota hopes to tap into the unifying energy that issues from the founding family to help get it through a tumultuous period in its history. Contrast that with Panasonic, which has chosen instead to stake its future on a break with its traditional ties to the founder, even dropping the Matsushita name. That's not to say either company is abandoning its corporate principles as laid out by their creators. On the contrary, in the face of unprecedented crisis, now more than ever they need to distill the essential principles of their founders and cut away the excesses that have calcified around them. These principles, shaped around new goals, should afford them a clearer view of the future.

Summary: Scaling Back to "Life-Size" Management

"Returning to one's roots" always sounds good, but one cannot gloss over the many scars that have formed on the corporate body over the years.

On June 23, 2009, this clarion call took symbolic form in Toyota's naming Akio Toyoda, direct descendent of Toyota Motor Corp. founder, Kiichiro, and son of former president Shoichiro Toyoda, to the company presidency. He assumes the reins at a time of severe crisis. In fiscal 2001, Toyota sales was far outpacing global growth in GPD. But by the end of fiscal 2009 (March), the automaker was posting its first deficits in 59 years. The losses are certain to mount further in 2010.

As a result, Toyota announced on August 28 that it was withdrawing from the long-standing automobile production partnership it had with General Motors since 1984 at the NUMMI plant in California. NUMMI had stood as a shining example of Japanese–US partnership in the automotive sector, but now that venture was bankrupt. With GM under Chapter 11 bankruptcy and national ownership, Toyota must face the challenges of overcoming the global recession as the lone leader of the automotive industry.

Here at another watershed moment in the company's history, "the Toyoda family serves as a rallying point for the entire group, for it has always been regarded as the company's centripetal force."

So commented former president, Hiroshi Okuda, who in 1995 replaced a different Toyoda family member, Tatsuro, as Toyota president. The same reverence shown toward the Toyoda family was expressed by subsequent non-Toyoda presidents in Fujio Cho and Katsuaki Watanabe upon seeing the youngest Toyoda scion, Akio, rise through the company ranks, from senior managing director to executive vice president. They had been priming him for an eventual ascension to the presidency. As an aggressive period of expansion and growth under Katsuaki Watanabe came to a screeching halt in 2008, the timing seemed right to bring forward a member of the founding family to spearhead a new business strategy.

With Toyota posting a 460 billion yen loss on its balance sheets for fiscal 2009 and a projected 850 billion yen loss for 2010, the young Akio must begin his tenure with bold reforms. But one advantage the 53-year-old Akio Toyoda wields, in addition to the family name, is plenty of energy; the energy to mobilize at least four powerful assets at his disposal and steer his ship through treacherous waters.

First, there is the "just-in-time" manufacturing system that continues to be improved upon over the years. Second, there is the gas-electric hybrid, Prius, and luxury Lexus brand, which have shaped a solid foundation for extending Toyota's lead in essential future technologies. Third are the joint ventures and partnerships with leading electronics makers, such as Panasonic, in growth areas such as batteries. Fourth, and perhaps most salient for this particular crisis, is strong cash-flow management made possible by rigorous financial discipline, which so far has not been too shaken by the global downturn.

Toyota is also a company that traces its management strength to teambuilding. Even with a young and relatively inexperienced leader, the company has the organizational horsepower to make a 90-degree turn toward new goals once a direction has been set. Toyota is legendary for having taken the traditional Japanese emphasis on teamwork in the workplace and putting that at the center of efforts to improve manufacturing quality and processes. As a flagship product, Toyota's Lexus brand automobiles always grace the top of J.D. Power and Associates rankings for quality. This is due to dynamic cooperative relationships in the workplace where unique and esoteric secrets of manufacturing know-how are shared and implemented. These are strengths being deployed at Toyota plants around the globe:

> It's not about sales volume or profits, but about what kinds of cars and price points will most satisfy the end user. We plan to rethink our "every segment and every direction" strategy we've pursued in recent years, and instead begin thinking in terms of matching actual conditions in every region of the world with more realistic, "life-size" management.

Akio Toyoda coined the phrase "life-size management" during his inauguration address as a way of encapsulating Toyota's new direction. The phrase was viewed as an indictment on the company's heretofore obsession with winning global leadership over GM, an effort that led to enormous excess capacity. With the US government in control of GM, plans are now to narrow its eight brands to four, including Chevrolet, Cadillac, and Buick. The revival plan also pares down sales targets from 8.35 million units in 2008 to just under 4 million in 2009. Toyota in 2008 recorded global sales of 8.97 million vehicles, putting it past GM as the world's leading automaker. But with the global recession's devastating impact on auto sales, Toyota must make a concerted effort to adjust its strategy downward to a humbler goal of 7.34 million vehicles in 2009: an 18 percent drop. Handing the company rein back to the founding family can be seen as marking an end to a heady rapid expansion strategy carried out since 2000, and a return to Toyota "prudentism."

Principal Ideas of Akio Toyoda

- Numbers don't come first. Customers and communities do.
- When in doubt, we must look to our foundations, and rediscover the "monozukuri" spirit.
- Apply "lifesize" management to real world conditions.

Toyota Motor Corp.

Established: August 28, 1937

Akio Toyoda, President and CEO

Head office: 1, Toyotacho, Toyota City, Aichi

http://www.toyota.co.jp/

Capital: 397,100 million yen (year ending March 2009)

Consolidated sales: 20,529,570 million yen

Consolidated operating profit: –461,011 million yen

Consolidated net profit: –436,937 million yen

Employees: 320,808

WORK STEADILY TOWARD OBJECTIVES, DON'T RUSH RESULTS

Sadayuki Sakakibara
President, CEO, COO and Representative Director
Toray Industries Inc.

Born March 1943 in Aichi Prefecture. Earned a master's degree from Nagoya University's School of Engineering in applied chemistry in 1967 and joined Toray (Toyo Rayon Co.) as a member of the central research lab. Served as head of the Business Planning Office and Export Management (1989), head of the First Business Planning Office (1994), managing director in charge of the First Business Planning Office and Second Business Planning Office (1996), senior managing director (1998), vice president with stints as head of the Personnel and Industrial Relations Division, corporate strategic planning, and the Technology Center, before his appointment as Toray president, COO, and representative director in June 2002. Appointed CEO in June 2004.

Learn from the Best to Become the Best

Considering the age of most of the companies featured in this book, Toray Industries seems to be a relative neophyte. Yet it has not needed a hundred years to grow into one of the leading textilemakers in the world, despite the big headstart its Western counterparts had in the industry. When the West was powering its way into the twentieth century on the back of the industrial revolution, churning out a wealth of groundbreaking "new textiles," the

Japanese textile sector was still firmly lodged in the eighteenth century, and viewed as lagging by some 20 to 30 years.

While the latter half of the nineteenth century saw the emergence of synthetic fibers in the West, Japan wouldn't begin domestic production of so-called "artificial silk" until 1918. Human-made silk was invented in France in 1881, with commercial application spreading quickly through Europe. In 1915, a professor at Yonezawa Technical High School (now Yamagata University's Engineering Department) named Itsuzo Hata developed an artificial silk, viscose rayon, for the first time in Japan.

"Silk" had until then only been produced by sericulture. Artificial silk was on the other hand made using wood pulp, which is of course a natural ingredient. But it required a human-made chemical process to turn it into yarn, hence the added prefix, "chemical" or "artificial" fiber.

The notion that one could "spin silk from trees" was viewed by people of the time as inconceivable. Ironically, the higher up one went in the chain of textile experts, the more dismissive was the reaction.

So one can only imagine the astonishment and excitement that was generated when the human-made silk was actually presented. The Japanese textile industry acted quickly to commercialize the product and sought to supplement it with further technology and knowledge from abroad.

Artificial silk, which came to be known as rayon, revolutionized the industry and spawned a galaxy of new businesses. Among them was Toyo Rayon (later renamed Toray), established in 1926 through funding by Mitsui & Company. No sooner had it begun rayon production in Shiga Prefecture when the upstart business saw orders soar through the roof. To meet the geometrically expanding demand, Toray built two more large-scale production sites in Ehime and Aichi prefectures.

The new material's sudden rise did spark voices of dissent among sericulturists worried that a long-cherished, traditional Japanese craft would fall by the wayside, if not creating distortions that would doom the textile industry as a whole. But instead, Japan's westernmost "Chugoku" region experienced an industrial renaissance as employment opportunities swelled, and as the general populace welcomed the human-made silk with open arms.

Consumption of rayon expanded unabated for some time afterward, prompting the Osaka edition of the *Mainichi* newspaper to boast in an article on March 30, 1927 that "the recent rise of artificial silk had brought about a revolution in the textile industry."

The Toyo Rayon Company grew at a rapid pace for the next quarter century and could have easily grown complacent, but instead displayed an eagerness to parlay success into newfound achievements. In 1951, after the acquisition of technical patents from DuPont, Toray entered into an agreement with the American chemical company to begin licensed production of nylon. Du Pont had sent into the world a premium nylon fiber dubbed Nylon 6-6, to which Toray's team of engineers quickly began applying their own expertise. When nylon first debuted on the market, it most commonly took the form of women's pantyhose and sold under the slogan, "Stronger than iron."

After expanding the nylon business, Toray and rival textile maker, Teijin Limited, procured know-how in polyester fiber from Britain's Imperial Chemical Industries (ICI), and started joint marketing of a synthetic material named "Tetoron®." Advanced properties such as ideal volume, strong fibrous backbone and an "easy care" nature earned the material high praise and widespread application in everything from clothing to interior materials such as car seats, seatbelts, tire cords, and nonwoven fabrics; all helping to improve the bottom line at both companies.

Toray's early stages in chemical material production of rayon was primarily driven by the introduction of basic technologies transferred from a British company, Courtaulds. But by the time they were churning out nylon products, the study and improve disposition so characteristic of Japanese industry led to more homegrown efforts, first with the development of a silk-imitating polyester fiber in 1964 called "Sillook®" followed that same year by "Toraylon®," an acrylic-based fiber. Both materials proved hits with consumers and commercial clients, as had Tetoron®, which had solved the perennial frustration of clothes shrinking in the wash.

Toray began in this way by seeking out the best technology in the world, and then applying that technology to a sustained development of convenient, high-grade materials. It was not a shortcut strategy to merely imitate and copy, but to acquire and adapt based on an honest appraisal of a material's strengths and weaknesses, and pour research energies aggressively into generating improvements. Credit this to a serious-minded temperament among the Japanese in general to focus on every detail and never be satisfied with the status quo.

Having amassed a solid technological base and a passion to innovate, Toray's onslaught of successful offerings, since it first diversified itself from a chemical fiber maker to a synthetic fiber producer, now extends over a vast array of products and applications, from Alcantara® synthetic suedes for automobile interiors to the carbon fiber Torayca® advanced composites used in aircrafts and construction materials, and the reverse osmosis membrane, Romenbra® for water treatment. Armed with such a replete portfolio, Toray is at last increasingly turning its attention to the great potential that dwells in markets overseas.

Quality Materials Lead to Quality Products

While cross-border acquisitions and alliances often create good business headlines, there is one partnership between two domestic companies that has quietly been at the heart of a major success story already treated in this book. It is a joint product development project between Toray and Fast Retailing, the firm that many observers feel now stands shoulder to shoulder with Toyota as the "face of Japan Inc." It would be no exaggeration to credit the naturally symbiotic relationship between Toray and Fast Retailing as behind the many major hit products spawned by Fast Retailing's prolific apparel chain, Uniqlo.

Toray announced that it would supply Uniqlo stores with 200 billion yen's worth of materials and manufactured products for five years to 2010, a practice that began a decade ago in 1999. Within this span, Toray has provided approximately 100 fleece jackets, the hit product that established Uniqlo in the minds of consumers nationwide in early 2000. Both companies have stated their desire to renew the relationship beyond 2010. Indeed, both have much to gain from a collaborative partnership that observers have described as mutually fair and lucrative, which includes personnel exchanges, joint R&D and information sharing. This active daily interaction has enabled the successful development of new materials and products for both companies, and created synergies in the form of integrated management for everything from materials development to product commercialization and sales along with efficiencies in replenishing shortages or holding down inventory excesses in both materials and finished goods.

Fast Retailing (Uniqlo) has designated Singapore as an important overseas base of operations from 2009, and is planning an aggressive store-opening campaign. Much of that success is riding on the stable development and supply of materials by Toray.

Alternately, Toray has placed its alliance with Fast Retailing high on its priority list. This can be best illustrated by Toray's dedication of one of its production lines to Uniqlo-specific materials such as the "Heat Tech series" that has given Uniqlo its biggest hit since fleece. Specifically, in the case of Heat Tech products for men, something called a "variant cross-section polyester made with cationic dyeable yarn" is employed to absorb and disperse perspiration, while in the women's versions, a mixture of rayon and milk protein is woven with fine acrylic fibers for a remarkable retention of heat and moisture.

Fast Retailing president Tadashi Yanai is effusive in his praise of Toray technology:

> We have made our cooperation with Toray a companywide priority effort to achieve a seamlessly integrated collaborative process, from development to sales. The new materials we're creating together is building the arsenal we need to compete globally.

In this sense, Toray rounds out the Uniqlo story in chapter 7 as the silent force behind the scenes sustaining Fast Retailing's high-octane run to global competitiveness. But it's not all rosy news for Toray. Amid the global economic downturn, fibers and textiles continue to account for as much as 40 percent of Toray's revenues, keeping the company highly dependent on its foundation business. Meanwhile, Japan imports more than 80 percent of its garments.

"Domestic garment makers have less than a 20 percent share of their own market," laments Sakakibara. "The reality is that the apparel industry relies heavily on low-cost products coming from China and other parts of Asia, a situation created by none other than the high cost of production or the distribution system in Japan."

Sakakibara sees this market dependence on imported sewn products as continuing to grow in the near term, while on the other hand exuding absolute confidence in the high quality of his company's products. Consumers will always welcome cheaper products. But he believes there is a recoil effect once quality dips below a bearable level, and that increasing consumer sophistication can be a long-term plus. Consumers do want great value, but they also want high-quality goods that they can cherish and use for a long time. Therein lies a growing need that Toray can meet and nurture.

Toray also attracted business headlines when it won an unprecedented 16-year exclusive contract with the US Boeing Company to produce carbon fiber composites for use in its upcoming 787 Dreamliner jetliners. The contract is projected to be worth approximately a trillion yen in materials that Toray will be supplying.

Behind this rare and exceptional contract is the influence of a considerably narrow "niche" business in this industry. Worldwide, carbon fiber is still a market of a few billion dollars, and is simply not lucrative enough for many companies to justify getting into, particularly when one recalls that a wide variety of companies did attempt to build businesses around it in the past, only to see the market fail to materialize and participants rapidly dwindle to just a handful. Currently, nearly three-quarters of the global share in carbon fiber is divided up among three Japanese materials makers, with Toray at 35 percent, Toho Tenax (a Teijin subsidiary) at 20 percent, and Mitsubishi Rayon at about 15 percent.

But if, as is the case with Boeing, other aviation companies or automakers begin to adopt the material and accelerate demand, a revitalized carbon-fiber market is well within expectations. This would represent a well-deserved payoff for Toray, which never abandoned the effort and instead has spent the past 50 years patiently developing the material.

"Yes, we have dedicated ourselves for nearly 50 years building the business to its current level, with most of that time spent in the red," says Sakakibara. "There have been five presidents at Toray before me, and each of them has tolerated the losses in this segment as a work in progress. As the sixth president, I feel fortunate to have been given the rein at a time the business is finally able to turn a profit in the hundreds of millions of dollars range."

This is a feat that would not have been possible under a short-term profit approach, but was the result of medium-to-long-range management vision and patience. Carbon fiber as a material has been around for quite some time, but may prove to be one of those inventions whose time has finally come.

With carbon fiber's potential to become a staple material in aviation and automotive industries, demand for a material previously deployed primarily in things such as golf club shafts and tennis rackets may start expanding geometrically. Great achievements are invariably built on the aggregate of hundreds of smaller successes and failures, and testify to the value of a sustained and dedicated effort backed by performance. Toray's carbon fiber has earned a level of trust that is warranting its large-scale use in cutting edge aviation and automotive technology.

But with a higher order of application comes a commensurate level of risk and responsibility. A tennis racket can snap in two at minimal cost and damage to the user. But when one is talking about jet airplanes in flight, or automobiles speeding along freeways at 65 miles an hour, a material that is anything less than failsafe is unacceptable.

R&D in these high-risk areas require massive outlays of capital investment. So one can imagine the considerable running costs and time that would accrue in making a product commercial ready, providing proper support services for it, and then making it profitable. All those added costs are reflected in the price of the product at the time of commercialization. If it is too high, consumer interest will fade quickly, regardless of how good the product may be. In an industry such as aviation, if a customer takes a short-term view to profitability, chances are that product has been rendered out of reach.

"Making a strong business case for carbon fiber has proven quite a challenge up until now, but we persisted under a firm conviction that it would be needed in the near future," Sakakibara continues. "So I too must take, as my predecessors did, a medium-to-long-term view and continue our efforts to make the highest-grade, highest-performing material possible. I feel that is our mandate as a leading materials maker."

Toray saw its net profits shrink in fiscal 2008, affected certainly by a delay in the start of carbon fiber production for the Boeing 787 jetliner, as well as the impact of continued declines in auto production around the world. When these issues resolve themselves, it is quite likely that Toray will begin reaping the rewards of its patience and persistence many times over.

Toray has overcome several crises since its founding in 1926. Yet the company has always prided itself on the resilience of its people, forged through the diligence, sense of loyalty and sacrifice, long-term perspective, and dogged persistence for which the Japanese worker is well-known. Sakakibara sees that as a function of being part and parcel of a larger whole:

We regard ourselves basically as a social entity. Our motto is to contribute to society through the creation of new values through our ideas, technologies and products. We are stakeholders in society. So we're never going to abandon that stance.

As a company philosophy, "contributing to society" can prove a tenuous effort to define and measure. What it essentially means is to contribute to the growth and betterment of society without being washed away with the changing currents of the times. It means having a strong enough sense of self and purpose to avoid becoming swept up by transient trends and succumbing to the temptation to pursue only immediate gains.

Like an individual member of society, a company must have the confidence to stay true to one's basic values and principles while also possessing enough self-esteem and confidence to seek changes for the better willingly. This applies as much to changes in the business environment as it does to those in one's personal or social lives.

Toray therefore marked the eightieth anniversary of its founding in 2006 by seeking to fortify its management foundation and establishing a long-term vision as: achieving dynamic evolution and sustainable growth en route to global leadership in advanced materials, while contributing to the development of society and environment through not only technology but also innovation in every aspect of operations, and creating new value for all stakeholders.

In short, it was a reclarification of a long-term management perspective that has consistently served as the bulwark of Toray efforts to date and will continue to steer and inform its activities going forward, regardless of what new and significant challenges arise.

Sure enough, the stiffest external challenge quite possibly in the company's history arrived two years later.

"In April of 2009, we launched a new medium-term business initiative (within our long-term plan) called 'Project IT-II (Innovation TORAY II)' in response to the steep challenges of the global downturn," Sakakibara announced. "Beginning with efforts to improve earnings by boosting total cost competitiveness in all of our businesses through additional internal restructuring, we aim to begin providing new solutions to many of the constraints to future economic growth that have surfaced in such areas as the environment, natural resource depletion and energy security, and of course in response to Japan's aging and contracting population. These will constitute a new focus for sustained growth going forward."

Sakakibara continues, "Increasing safety, promoting environmental protection, and ensuring ethical and responsible corporate behavior are high- priority management issues. In the environmental sphere, for example, with our focus on recycling efforts through our ECODREAM program, we are aggressively working toward the eventual realization of a fully sustainable, eco-friendly society."

Overseas Growth Key to Building Trust

Sadayuki Sakakibara beams confidently about his company's ability to endure the current worldwide economic debacle, and perhaps emerge stronger for it. And why not? He runs a well-diversified multinational corporation that operates in 21 countries and regions and is Japan's biggest textile maker as well as the global leader in carbon-fiber production. Most of all, Sakakibara's optimism is a manifestation of his high expectations toward consumers and his own deep sense of responsibility:

> Even a global downturn of unprecedented proportions is not going to force us to rethink the importance and value of our foundation business in textile and fibers. We may have to work hard to rationalize global production further, but we have no plans to begin contracting or abandoning any of our products.

Indeed, Toray's foundation businesses extend beyond textiles and fibers to also include plastics and chemicals, and is working tirelessly to establish a stable base of revenues through global expansion, advancing its downstream and processing businesses, and becoming what it calls a "new value creator."

Toray's corporate philosophy of "contributing to society through the creation of new value" is based on a plan to strengthen core technologies, and R&D to create the "advanced materials" that best reflect the ongoing changes in people's lives. While Toray does have a vast array of cutting edge materials in development, two that hold great promise in the near-term are so-called "information and tele-communication-related materials" and "advanced composites."

The carbon fiber composites Toray is supplying to Boeing for its 787 Jetliner is a material that is 10 times more robust than steel, yet has 75 percent less weight. This would also make it more fuel-efficient. It is also touted as highly heat resistant and won't rust like steel. It is also easier to produce carbon fiber, so if used liberally in jet airplanes, it could greatly reduce production times.

Much of the same can be said for its use in automobiles, where the benefits of easier assembly processes, reduced production times and improved fuel efficiency could be revolutionary. So it is no wonder that amid rising concerns about environmental degradation and global warming that much attention and hope is being invested in the next "dream" material.

Life sciences and environment, particularly water treatment are two fields where Toray is looking to expand revenues beyond its foundational business areas after 2010, and the company has made clear a strategy that includes acquisitions and joint ventures.

Most of these initiatives are slated to be carried out over the medium-to-long term, and Toray holds no illusions about the need to reap some immediate results. But it is precisely this medium-to-long-term outlook that has carried the company through rough and peaceful times alike throughout its 80-year history. Like the worn Western adage, "haste makes waste," a Japanese version uttered with greater frequency goes: "when in a hurry, take the long route." It seems to sum up the management stance at Toray. Indeed, there are many cases of Japanese companies, including those treated in this book, for which hasty expansion led to failure. South Korea, for example, has often been viewed as a logical first place to get a foothold in overseas operations because of many market similarities and physical proximity. Yet considerable cultural differences, not to mention the checkered history between the two countries, are also reflected in widely disparate business philosophies that have often been overlooked.

Sakakibara even used the opportunity of a 2009 keynote address at a symposium honoring South Korean President Lee Myung-bak to offer a critique of basic differences in the two countries' managerial styles.

It seems a natural part of the business temperament in Korea to want to do everything as quickly as possible. Many business plans are crafted around short-term results and consumed with short-term profits, which makes decision making, when viewed from a Japanese managerial standpoint, appear very quick, even reckless.

Sakakibara also spoke of a prevailing belief among Korean managers that capital investment in a market must always be grandiose, in contrast to Japanese managers, who may establish a base in Korea, for example, but won't invest a disproportionate amount of resources there because it is only part of a larger global expansion strategy that includes the home market. In short, they seek more regional balance, all the while keeping their eye on domestic demand.

Conversely, this philosophy strikes Korean managers as decision making that runs at glacial speed. Even among Asian neighbors, business philosophies can be worlds apart.

"Japanese synthetic fiber makers rushed to South Korea in the late 1970s in search of the next big market," says Sakakibara. "But with the exception of Toray, nearly all have since pulled out, demonstrating how difficult it is for Japanese companies to succeed in different settings like Korea.

"Building mutual trust among top managers also proved challenging, with most Japanese companies ending up clashing with their partners over meager profits that hampered true cooperation. Labor unions in Korea are also much more powerful than their counterparts in Japan, and many Japanese firms couldn't stomach the frequency of worker strikes."

While Japanese companies fled the country in rapid succession, Toray stuck it out.

"In the end, we never had to alter our medium-to-long-term approach to business," Sakakibara confides. "From the outset, we tried not to dwell on short-term pursuit of profits, and we had to make sure our Korean partners fully understood that. We held a lot of conversations, but over time, things began to naturally gel between us. Now we have built an unwavering foundation of trust and cooperation."

New Materials to Generate New Products

Toray is looking for other ways to survive the recession by scaling new heights. One of those efforts is in its partnership with sportswear maker, Goldwin Inc.

Goldwin is known for having established an environmentally friendly recycling system whereby consumers can return clothes they have purchased once they are ready to dispose of them. While this trend to recycle materials and return them to production lines has been in effect for some time, the company plans to expand and accelerate the activity from the fall of 2009.

This is because of Toray's own ECODREAM recycling system, which Goldwin plans to use to enlarge the range of recyclable materials with systems dedicated to recovering polyester and nylon products. Designing and building products with recyclable components has already become a given in the automotive and consumer appliance industries, and will increasingly hold sway over corporate images in the apparel industry as well.

The repeated recycling of energy and resources that can contribute to suppression of CO_2 emissions and conservation is treated as a major theme of the partnership between Toray and Goldwin, to be actualized through corporate initiative and consumer cooperation. For its part, Goldwin hopes to build its image as a health and eco-conscious member of society through its sportswear and green production.

"Deploying our ECODREAM system enables Goldwin to reduce energy consumption by about 70 percent in comparison to manufacturing oil-based Nylon 6," says Sakakibara about Toray's world-class chemical recycling technology. "Similarly, we've also demonstrated that the system reduces CO_2 emissions by 70 percent as well. This is possible because it breaks products down to their particle level. Plus you get the same high purity levels as when producing from petroleum already, and that should only improve as we continue to advance the technology."

In June of 2008, Toray completed the construction of a state-of-the-art climate chamber called "Technorama G2" in Nantong, China. The facility's main feature is its ability to simulate a wide variety of climatic phenomenon around the world from blizzard-prone areas to dry desert and humid tropical jungle.

The R&D facility allows Toray to measure and evaluate changes to clothing fibers when moved between different climactic environments, and freely set up a wide range of simulated experimental conditions, such as suddenly going from outdoor summer heat to a highly air-conditioned room, or from a heated automobile to a frigid and snowy winter world outside.

The research also contributes to R&D of other materials, including environment-responsive resins and textiles for automotive use.

Says Sakakibara:

Whether you're in research or sales, we endeavor to create an atmosphere that encourages everyone to keep their antennae tuned to capturing all sorts of information, which can lead to great new ideas. So naturally, when it comes to people, we want people who won't be "yes men" but are enthusiastic about sharing their personal thoughts and insights; people who like to set goals in the face of challenges, and who can introduce new and different perspectives. So we want to continue to create a work environment that values those types of traits, and I believe that to be one of my most important jobs as president.

It is Sakakibara's long-term patience and flexible mind that are helping to keep Toray a lively and vigorous place to work, from the headquarters to research labs and factories.

Toray has also designated the medical sector as one of its key "strategically developing businesses" under a motto of providing "advanced high-quality medicine" beginning with artificial organs and extending to medical equipment and even pharmaceutical products.

Specifically, this includes sales and ongoing R&D in medical instrumentation materials such as surgical gloves, catheters, and devices such as the artificial kidney dialysis device "Filterizer®"; the emergency and intensive care treatment blood purifier, Toraymixin®; a natural interferon-beta preparation for treating chronic hepatitis C, Feron®; and medical support hose used in prevention and post-op rehabilitation for varicose veins and lymphedema.

Among these, it is the medical support hose designed to improve blood circulation in the legs that was launched in 2005, which has received the most attention, particularly in preventing "economy-class syndrome" or deep-vein thrombosis. The product dubbed "Fine Support" is easy to put on, works to reduce foot swelling, and uses Toray's popular moisture-absorbing nylon filament, TOREX® QUUP®.

Toray's contributions to the life sciences have led to several breakthroughs. For example, Toray continued to develop a core technology used in its 1985 biotech product, Feron® (a natural interferon preparation for chronic hepatitis type B and C), resulting in what promises to be the world's first hepatitis C vaccine.

Toray's Life Sciences business is generating landmark drugs and treatments on par with a full-fledged pharmaceutical maker, while pioneering the fusion of biotechnology and nanotechnology. In 2006, Toray entered DNA chip construction for genetic testing and analysis, an area heralded as the future of tailor-made medicine. In less than five years, Toray chips have grown 100 times in their sensitivity to detect gene information. The future looks bright for Toray in this bio-tools sphere as the innovative company expands its portfolio, reputation, and contribution to leading cancer, immunity system, and metabolic syndrome research.

Toray is also getting involved in renovating and retrofitting medical facilities with materials and equipment through a subsidiary to better meet today's realities, such as the need to hold down the mounting energy consumption of medical devices as they increase in sophistication.

Toray has earned strong support for its renovation proposals designed to make buildings not only function more efficiently but are environmentally friendly and reduce operational costs.

For example, Toray is confident in its ability to improve building safety by using its proud carbon fiber in slabs to reinforce structural elements against increased loads or earthquakes, or in seismic flooring. Toray materials are being used to great effect in reducing noise, vibration, and electromagnetic wave leakages in hospitals.

More sophisticated technologies and rigorous quality management abilities are increasingly being called into demand in areas that have an impact on the quality of human life. Toray is not looking to parlay its core strengths into more diversified finished products simply to gain access to new market segments, but instead believes it a natural outgrowth of its corporate mandate to seek sustained growth by contributing to society through the creation of new values.

Not hurrying results, living by a medium-to-long-term perspective and creating a climate for active research are what have largely contributed to Toray's place in the world today. If empires cannot be created overnight, then neither can companies whose products are relied upon in the daily lives of people around the world. Even amid a global economic maelstrom that is leaving no boats or harbors unscathed, Toray president Sakakibara, like his predecessors, remains fixed on the horizon.

Summary: Materials for a New Age

Toray Industries built the synthetic fiber and textile business in Japan, growing into a high-earnings blue-chip company that is now among the global leaders in its industry. What drove the company were strong technologies enabling a sustained new materials development effort under a sense of mission to "aim to be the world's leader in advanced materials." Toray did not limit its portfolio to synthetic fibers but deployed its technological strength to develop materials applicable in a wide range of industries, from plastic resins and information and telecommunication-related materials to carbon-fiber composites and water processing. As mentioned, Toray's persistence in developing its carbon-fiber materials is at last paying dividends. The company has become the world number one producer of carbon fiber as a new structural material for use in airplanes and automobiles. Toray also moved quickly to capitalize on overseas expansion opportunities and now operates in 21 countries and regions through 225 group companies.

Toray was founded in 1926 as a subsidiary of Mitsui & Co. to produce a human-made replacement for silk in the form of rayon. In 1942, Toray succeeded in developing a spinning fiber called Nylon 6. Toray's partnership with the US DuPont Company in 1951 set it on a course as a fully fledged synthetic fiber and textiles business, and watched its nylon business expand dramatically. That was followed in 1957 by its introduction of a groundbreaking polyester material called Tetoron® developed together rival materials maker Teijin Limited and with the help of technology imported from the British Imperial Chemicals Industries. This enabled Toray to strike out on its own proprietary development of materials beginning with the acrylic fiber, Torayon®. Producing the three major synthetic textiles allowed it to grow into a comprehensive synthetic materials maker and rank among Japan's top high-earning companies as it headed toward its silver anniversary.

Toray's first big hurdle came in the 1970s when overproduction coupled with a rising yen hurt exports, and sent the company into its first ever phase of retraction and restructuring, prompting Toray to consider diversifying its business portfolio to supplement its foundation business. The decision was made to move into plastics and polyester film, which paid off in such products as Sillook®, a silk-like polyester fiber, a new synthetic leather called "Ecsaine®," and the carbon fiber, Torayca®. When domestic demand for synthetic materials and export markets began to taper off in the 1970s, Toray began shifting its production bases for synthetic materials such as Tetoron® to overseas locations such as southeast Asia, eventually equaling domestic production volume. Toray has also built on its strong technological base in materials with offerings in life sciences and environment sectors, including a new compound (PEG-interferon beta) to treat hepatitis C, and a reverse-osmosis membrane for seawater desalination. Demand for both products is already high, and Toray hopes to make such advanced materials account for 60 percent of sales by about 2015.

It was one of Sakakibara's predecessors, current honorary chairman Katsunosuke Maeda, who inaugurated a decade of change from 1987 centered around the restructuring of the company's foundation business and setting out on a course of diversification into nontextile areas. Maeda asserted that despite an industrywide contraction in synthetic fiber production, Toray should continue to reap as much of "the spoils" that remained in the market while aggressively seeking new growth in new fields.

Sadayuki Sakakibara rose to the presidency in 2002 from the technocratic ranks as an applied sciences engineer developing carbon fiber under the tutelage of earlier R&D chief Yoshikazu Ito who would also become company president. Ito describes Sakakibara as someone who absorbed Toray's technocentric DNA. But Sakakibara would inherit financial woes upon taking the top office, stemming from a deteriorating synthetic fiber market worldwide, which left Toray badly exposed to the Asian currency crisis and the collapse of the IT bubble. The burden of servicing that debt put Toray in the red for the year ending March 2002, prompting Katsunouske Maeda to be reinstated as CEO so that he could team up with the fledgling president Sakakibara and take the necessary cost-cutting and reform measures to put the company back on track. After formulating a 10-point roadmap and long-term corporate vision called "Action Program-New TORAY21," designed to transform the company for the twenty-first century, Sakakibara aggressively pushed to create foundations for new growth in advanced materials where Toray could strive for global leadership. One of those was carbon fiber.

When demand for carbon fiber shot up as a new industrial material for the aviation and automotive sectors, Toray and rivals ramped up output and added new production lines. Then the global economic recession hit in the fall of 2008. Boeing decided to delay production of its 787 jetliner, and the double-digit growth in demand for carbon fiber receded like water at low tide. Production facilities Toray had built around the world had to be put on hold, and plans for new production lines were frozen. Projected operating profits from the carbon-fiber business plummeted from some eight billion yen a year to zero.

Sakakibara has been through this before. But now he is an even more seasoned captain at the helm.

"The market will return," he beams confidently. "We'll be there when it does."

For the time being, Toray will look to increase earnings elsewhere while continuing the never-ending work of adding to its stockpile of new products and technologies. A little patience and ingenuity may be all that are needed for Toray to weather this new storm. Fortunately for Toray, those are two of the company's patented traits.

Principal Ideas of Sadayuki Sakakibara

- Contribute to society through the persistent creation of new values.
- Management vision and patience pays off in the long run.
- Great achievements are built on the aggregate of hundreds of smaller successes.

Toray Industries Inc.

Established: January 12, 1926

Sadayuki Sakakibara, CEO, COO, President and Representative Director

Head office: 2-1-1, Nihonbashi-muromachi, Chuo-ku, Tokyo

http://www.toray.com/

Capital: 534,838 million yen (year ending March 2009)

Consolidated sales: 1,471,561 million yen

Consolidated operating profit: 36,006 million yen

Consolidated net profit: −16,326 million yen

Consolidated employees: 37,924

EPILOGUE

The financial crisis that began in the US in the fall of 2008 before sweeping across the globe is likely to redraw the economic map of the world. While the advanced industrialized nations of Europe, the US, and Japan all plunged in unison into minus growth, the crisis has not severely shaken the foundations of emerging economic powerhouses like China and India. The center of economic gravity in the world is shifting: from the US to Asia. The importance of newly industrializing economies in global equity markets continues to rise, as does the market value of many of their companies.

In this environment, Japanese firms, too, have slipped in the rankings. But as the losses owing to the rupture of the credit bubble in the US and around the world reach astronomical figures in financial markets, there are many manufacturing-based companies that face opportunities for an early recovery thanks to their proximity to and investment in real economies—the physical economy as opposed to the paper economy centering on lifestyle, food, software, games and high-quality manufactured products—and this has served to reaffirm the strength of their presence and tangible technologies in burgeoning Asian markets.

Even as the world's automakers have all fallen into financial straits owing to slumping global car sales, Toyota and Honda are running away with the global hybrid-vehicle market, virtually dividing it between them. Panasonic is bolstering sales of its consumer appliances to emerging countries, while merging with Sanyo Electric in the digital environment to surge ahead in key future technologies such as lithium-ion and solar batteries. Nintendo continues to set the global standard in home videogame entertainment, and Japanese cosmetics giant Shiseido is expanding its vision of feminine beauty across Asia. Kirin and Suntory's recently announced merger is sure to bring a key major industrial realignment and structural changes to the alcohol and beverage sector, with the financial crisis having served as a catalyst. One byproduct of the crisis that is sure to come about is a strengthening of reform plans among top Japanese managers around new mid-to-long-term views of their business. The 15 corporations and their managers described in this book are only a pared-down list of what I believe are some—but not all—of the intrinsically strong private companies from Japan. With a combined total of more than 1,200 years in business, they define the past, present, and future of Japanese industry without a doubt.

While I have tried to cover a broad range of sectors in my selection, a quick look at the biggest rivals of most these companies would automatically expand the list of Japanese firms by a factor of two or even three. But what I hope this book accomplishes in at least an encapsulated way is to impart to you the "true worth" behind the leading firms of Japan; by the time the dust settles on this global financial crisis, and the world seems ready to move forward into the future, these will be 15 companies and managers to watch.

BIBLIOGRAPHY

gendai.net, April 6, 2009, Gendai net.

Hasegawa, Yozo. *Clean Car Wars*. Chuokoron-Shinsha, Inc., 2008. (English edition published Wiley & Sons, Pte. Ltd., 2008).

——. *Kono Jigyo ni Kakeru* (Betting on This Business). Nikkei Publishing Inc., 2004.

——. *Shacho no Shigoto-ho: Nobiru Shaiin o Tsukuru Keieisha no Hasso* (President Work Methods: How Top Managers Foster Better Employees). Kodansha Ltd., 2008.

Iida, Ryo. *Sekai no Dokonimonai Kaisha o Tsukuru!* (Build a Globally Unique Company!). Soshisha Publishing Co. Ltd., 2007.

Inoguchi, Osamichi. *Kirin no Ryugi* (Kirin Way). PRESIDENT Inc., 2007.

Inoue, Masahiro, Fujio Onishi, and Takaaki Muramatsu. *Toray*. ShuppanBunkaSha Corp., 2008.

Inoue, Osamu. *Nintendo "Odoroki" o Umu Hoteishiki* (Nintendo: Formula for Surprise). Nikkei Publishing Inc., 2009.

Kawakami, Seiichi, Takashi Nagai, and Hiroshi Saji. *Kirin Beer*. Shuppan-BunkaSha Corp., 2008.

Kawashima, Yoko. *Shiseido Brand*. Aspect Corporation, 2007.

Kunitomo, Ryuichi. *Shohisha Shinri wa Uniqlo ni Kike!* (The Consumer Mind? Ask Uniqlo!). PHP Research Institute, Inc., 2001.

Mizuno, Takushi. *Shiseido Sendenbu Nikki* (A Diary of the Shiseido Advertising Division). Bungeishunju Ltd., 2008.

Mogi, Yuzaburo. *Kikkoman no Gurobaru Keiei* (Kikkoman Global Management). Japan Productivity Center Publication, 2007.

Nagai, Takashi. *Biiru Saishu Senso* (The Last Beer Battle). Nikkei Publishing Inc., 2006.

NHK Reporting Team. *Shin-Nittetsu vs. Mittal* (Nippon Steel vs. Mittal). Diamond Inc., 2007.

Nikkei Business, March 3, 2008 issue, Nikkei Business Publications, Inc.

Nikkei Publishing Inc. *Canon-Shiki* (Canon Mode). 2004.

Nishikawa, Ryujin. *0 Yen de Oku o Kasegu!* (Earning a Million from Zero Yen!). Magazine House, Ltd., 2008.

Ogata, Tomoyuki. *Futari no Ryutsu Kakumei* (The Two-Man Distribution Revolution). Nikkei Business Publications, Inc., 1999.

——. *Masao Ogura: Keieigaku* (Masao Ogura's Business Science). Nikkei Business Publications, Inc., 1999.

Osada, Takahito. *The Panasonic Way.* PRESIDENT Inc., 2006.

Sakane, Masahiro. *Kagiri nai Dantotsu Keiei no Chosen* (The Challenge of "Dantotsu" Management). JUSE Press, Ltd., 2009.

Sakazume, Ichiro. *Mitarai Fujio Canon-Ryu Genbashugi* (Fujio Mitarai's Canon-style "Genba-ism"). Toyo Keizai, Inc., 2004.

Sankei News, July 26, 2008, The Sankei Shimbun & Sankei Digital.

Sato, Masaaki. *Toyota no Sutorateji* (Toyota Strategy). Bungeishunju Ltd., 2009.

Shibai, Yoshihiro. *Monozukuri ni Yume o Egaku* (Shaping a Manufacturer's Dream). Shinpusha Co., Ltd., 2005.

Suzuki, Toshifumi. *Chosen: Waga Roman* (Our Romantic Challenge). Nikkei Publishing Inc., 2008.

——. *Shobai no Sozo* (The Creation of Business). Kodansha Ltd., 2003.

Takeda, Kunio. *Ochikobore Takeda o Kaeru* (Changing a Laggard Takeda). Nikkei Publishing Inc., 2005.

Takeuchi, Ichimasa. *Saraba Matsushita! Tanjo Panasonic* (Farewell Matsushita, Hello Panasonic!). Pal Publishing, 2008.

Usiminas group. *Ujiminas Kaisoroku* (Usiminas Memoirs).

Yanai, Tadashi. *Issho Kyuhai* (1 Win, 9 Losses). Shinchosha Publishing Co., Ltd., 2003.

INDEX